MW00510662

KJV DEVOTIONAL

for Men

NICK HARRISON

HARVEST HOUSE PUBLISHERS
EUGENE, OREGON

All Scripture quotations are taken from the King James Version of the Bible.

Cover design by Dugan Design Group
Cover photo © Eberhard Grossgasteiger / Unsplash
Interior design by KUHN Design Group

For bulk, special sales, or ministry purchases, please call 1 (800) 547-8979.
Email: Customerservice@hhpbooks.com

M is a federally registered trademark of the Hawkins Children's LLC. Harvest House Publishers, Inc., is the exclusive licensee of the trademark.

KJV Devotional for Men

Copyright © 2022 by Harvest House Publishers
Published by Harvest House Publishers
Eugene, Oregon 97408
www.harvesthousepublishers.com

ISBN 978-0-7369-8487-4 (hardcover)
ISBN 978-0-7369-8489-8 (eBook)

Printed in China

22 23 24 25 26 27 28 29 30 / RDS / 10 9 8 7 6 5 4 3 2

INTRODUCTION

You've probably picked up this book of devotions for men because you were drawn to the fact that it features the King James Version of the Bible. If so, you're one of the millions of Bible lovers who still prefer the beauty and classic rhythms of this four-hundred-year-old translation of the Bible to the many new translations or paraphrases of God's Word.

The "Authorized" King James Version of the Bible was the result of King James I of England's direction that a translation of the Bible be readied for the Church of England. Seven years later, after the painstaking work of more than fifty qualified men, the new Bible was published—not as the King James Version or Authorized Version (that designation would come two centuries later) but as the more cumbersome *The Holy Bible, Conteyning the Old Testament, and the New: Newly Translated Out of the Originall Tongues: & with the Former Translations Diligently Compared and Revised by His Majesties Speciall Comandement.*

It should be noted that all the translators were well aware of the gravity of their task. All were university graduates—many from Oxford and Cambridge. With precision, they diligently crafted the monumental book that has served generation after generation of Christian believers.

Some of the fans of the KJV include Pulitzer Prize–winning author Eudora Welty, who has written, "How many of us, the South's writers-to-be of my generation, were blessed in one way or another, if not blessed alike, in not having gone deprived of the King James Version of the Bible. Its cadence entered into our ears and our memories for good." Indeed, she speaks not just for those from the American South but for fans of the KJV here and abroad, not all of whom were religious people.

Even skeptic and Nobel Prize winner George Bernard Shaw sang its praises.

The translation was extraordinarily well done because to the translators what they were translating was not merely a curious collection of ancient books written by different authors in different stages of culture, but the word of God divinely revealed through His chosen and expressly inspired scribes. In this conviction they carried out their work with boundless reverence and care and achieved a beautifully artistic result...they made a translation so magnificent that to this day the common human Britisher or citizen of the United States of North America accepts and worships it as a single book by a single author, the book being the Book of Books and the author being God.

The great British statesman Winston Churchill opined, "The scholars who produced this masterpiece [the King James Bible] are mostly unknown and unremembered. But they forged an enduring link, literary and religious, between the English-speaking people of the world."

Today, the King James Version of the Bible remains extremely popular, standing firm against the plethora of additional translations. In fact, it is still the second-best-selling version, after the New International Version.

If you still remember the Scriptures you memorized from the KJV in your youth and can't quite see the advantage of the sometimes awkward phrasing of newer versions, I think you'll find solace, support, and guidance as you enjoy time with the Lord and with His Word, the King James Version of the Bible.

A Man's Eyes

I will set no wicked thing before mine eyes (PSALM 101:3).

The light of the body is the eye: if therefore thine eye be single, thy whole body shall be full of light. But if thine eye be evil, thy whole body shall be full of darkness (MATTHEW 6:22-23).

A man's eyes take in many sights on any given day. But some of those sights can lead a man into sin if he doesn't police his vision. An envious eye may reveal a covetous heart. A critical eye may indicate prejudice. A roving eye may harbor adulterous desires. Every Christian man must determine that he will "set no wicked thing" before his eyes. Rather, he must affirm that his eyes are singularly focused on light, not the darkness of sin.

"Our eyes, when gazing on sinful objects, are out of their calling, and out of God's keeping." —THOMAS FULLER

Learning to Enjoy Silence

Be still, and know that I am God (Psalm 46:10).

The presence of the Lord is everywhere but is better perceived in stillness. The world around us is geared toward noise, activity, and ambition. To be still and know that He is God requires that we make time for stillness.

Perhaps in prayer we have told God we want to hear His voice; we want to know how to make wise decisions, but we sense no reply. Is it because we find listening to God in silence uncomfortable? We reason that we should be up and about *doing* rather than sitting still in silence.

All the while God has answers to our every question, but He wants us to seek the answers in communion with Him—often *silent* communion. The riches from God's treasury are often mined from silent canyons, not amid the clamor of busyness.

Be assured, if we will not search out stillness, neither will it search us out.

"There is hardly ever a complete silence in our soul. God is whispering to us well-nigh incessantly. Whenever the sounds of the world die out in the soul, or sink low, then we hear these whisperings of God." —Frederick W. Faber

LOVE ONE ANOTHER

This is my commandment, That ye love one another, as I have loved you (JOHN 15:12).

How do we love others? Basically, we're *there* for them. We learn to know them as we would like to be known by them. We engage them by drawing out their history. We open a line of communication that allows them to trust us as friends, not just acquaintances.

Jesus was with His disciples for a good three years. Daily they saw His love toward others as He healed the sick, fed the multitudes, and in the grandest display of love, died on the cross for the sins of all. This tells us that love, above all, is sacrificially giving to others freely.

Love, then, isn't hard. It's thinking of others in the way Jesus thinks of us.

"If we do not love one another, we certainly shall not have much power with God in prayer." —D.L. MOODY

Forgiven and Forgiving

Be ye kind one to another, tenderhearted, forgiving one another, even as God for Christ's sake hath forgiven you (EPHESIANS 4:32).

The man who thinks he has no need for forgiveness is a lost man. The Christian man is one who has seen the true depth of his sin toward God and toward others. Forgiveness is a primary need if he is ever to experience God and restore fellowship with a person who needs his forgiveness.

A regular inventory of our relationships should reveal if there's an offense toward God or others that we must make right. When we see an offense either against us or toward another, it's time to allow our hearts to become tender and exercise forgiveness, confession, and even restitution, if necessary. A forgiven Christian man has removed a heavy burden indeed.

"To be a Christian means to forgive the inexcusable, because God has forgiven the inexcusable in you." —C.S. LEWIS

The Thoughts of a Godly Man

For as he thinketh in his heart, so is he (Proverbs 23:7).

For most men, our thoughts are often random, wandering here and there based on external circumstances. We sometimes forget that our thoughts are the sum total of who we are. Take away our thought life and we are just an empty shell.

God cares about our thoughts. He would have us daily submit our minds to Him and center our thoughts on His will. Far too often the thoughts of an undisciplined mind take us in directions we don't want to go. Every man must identify the recurring thoughts that turn into temptations and reroute them to the mind's recycle bin. Evil or negative thoughts must be replaced by creative thoughts that are positive and God-affirming. For most men, this involves retraining our brains, and with the Holy Spirit as our Helper, we can learn to think rightly.

"Imagination is the hotbed where this sin is too often hatched. Guard your thoughts, and there will be little fear about your actions." —J.C. Ryle

Natural Evangelism

Though I preach the gospel, I have nothing to glory of: for necessity is laid upon me; yea, woe is unto me, if I preach not the gospel! (1 Corinthians 9:16).

God calls every man to share the good news of the gospel in whatever way he is gifted to do so. For many, some ways of evangelism seem forced and unnatural, but a gifted man will find creative and effective ways to simply share with others. The problem many men have is they don't look expectantly for God to open the door of opportunity to share the gospel.

Ask God to bring the right person who needs to hear about Christ your way and respond naturally as to how God has worked with you. Let nothing feel forced; simply share and follow up with private prayer for the person in need.

"The question of speaking to souls is a question of personal love to the Lord Jesus Christ. Do not say you have no gift for it. Do you love Christ? If so, you will never lose an opportunity of speaking a word for Him." —G.V. Wigram

EDIFYING THE CHURCH

Even so ye, forasmuch as ye are zealous of spiritual gifts, seek that ye may excel to the edifying of the church (1 CORINTHIANS 14:12).

The word we translate as "church" literally means "called out" ones. And within the church of God's "called out" ones is a love every Christian man must have. For to love Christ must also mean to love His bride. And every man has some gift to bring to edify his fellow believers. The work may be small or large, but whatever the task, God has appointed it to be accomplished.

Have you discovered how God wants to use you and your spiritual gifts to edify your fellow believers? Be zealous of spiritual gifts and pray for an understanding of the way God plans to use you. Don't shrink back from giving to the church, for in giving, you will also receive.

"A spiritual gift is a supernaturally designed ability granted to every believer by which the Holy Spirit ministers to the body of Christ. A spiritual gift cannot be earned, pursued or worked up. It is merely 'received' through the grace of God." —JOHN MACARTHUR

Resisting the Enemy

Submit yourselves therefore to God. Resist the devil, and he will flee from you (JAMES 4:7).

Every Christian man is Satan's target. This brutal enemy has plans to render men ineffective in their personal life—and in their spiritual life. However, no man is left unguarded by God in the battle. Safety is found in submitting entirely to God and resisting the specific influences Satan has devised to take you down.

Resisting must begin with the very first hint of temptation. If we don't resist early, we're more likely to fall into Satan's trap. The best warriors have learned how to identify their enemy and defeat him. So must every man. Be strong in the Lord. Submit to God. Resist the enemy at every turn—and watch him flee.

"Many men have no heart to resist a temptation. No sooner does Satan come with his solicitations—but they yield...He is a valorous Christian who brandishes the sword against Satan, and will rather die than yield. The heroic spirit of a saint is never more seen than in a battlefield, when he is fighting with the red dragon—and by the power of faith puts the devil to flight!" —THOMAS WATSON

FRIENDSHIP

A friend loveth at all times, and a brother is born for adversity (PROVERBS 17:17).

Many Christian men lament their lack of deep friendships with other men. They read of the closeness of David and Jonathan and wish for something like that in their own lives. Friendship, like so much else, is a gift of God. A man with no friends misses out on a key relationship in spiritual growth. For the love of a friend reveals the love of God, and during times of adversity, a true friend becomes God with skin. To have friends, one must show himself friendly. To enlarge one's circle of friends begins with asking God for the gift of friends. It then requires us to move out of our comfort zones and reach out, perhaps to those we sense are in need of friends too.

The strength of a church is largely determined by the extent of the friendships within the fellowship of the church.

"There is a brotherhood within the body of believers, and the Lord Jesus Christ is the common denominator. Friendship and fellowship are the legal tender among believers."
—J. VERNON MCGEE

SERVANTHOOD

Whosoever of you will be the chiefest, shall be servant of all (MARK 10:44).

By love serve one another (GALATIANS 5:13).

In God's upside-down economy, the way up is down. The way to be a "chief" is to become a servant. Laying down one's life for others is inherent in the Christian life, and the most spiritual men are those who serve others.

How can one serve? By noticing and meeting needs that are within your ability to meet. A servant's eyes are always alert for the needs of the one served. And because such alertness isn't natural, we must train ourselves to be servants. One way to become better servants is to consider Christ, who, though Lord of all, reduced Himself to become a servant of all. In His humility, He was exalted. Serve others and the reward will be yours.

"The secret of abundant helpfulness, is found in the desire to be a help, a blessing, to all we meet. We begin to be like Christ only when we begin to wish to be helpful. Where this desire is ever dominant, the life is an unceasing benediction. Rivers of water are pouring out from it continually to bless the world."
—J. R. MILLER

The Secure Man

Watch ye, stand fast in the faith, quit you like men, be strong
(1 Corinthians 16:13).

Our source of strength as men is from the God who first created us, now empowers us, and will eventually welcome us to a heavenly home in His presence. While we're here in this earthen body, let's be not just men but *strong* men. Men of true faith; virtuous men who stand up for right and object when we see wrong. Let us be men who are possessed by the Spirit of God.

Let us be active men. Passivity in Christian men is a shame. And sadly, it can be contagious. But so can strength become contagious when true men are willing to be counted as righteous, denying evil and promoting good.

Be strong in the day at hand. Be a man.

"Christianity makes men, not babes. Adorn the doctrine of Christ by your manliness. In the Church, in the world, in business, in conversation, in prosperity, and adversity, [act] like men! Let no man despise you; and let no man despise the Gospel because of you." —Horatius Bonar

Role Models

Be ye followers of me, even as I also am of Christ (1 Corinthians 11:1).

*Ye are our epistle written in our hearts, known and read of all
men* (2 Corinthians 3:2).

We never know who's watching us. As Paul notes,
we are all epistles, read by those we meet along
the way. Even this very day, someone may be influenced
by observing how we react to an unexpected circumstance. Paul could encourage the recipients of his letters
to follow his example. Why? Because he followed Christ.

For each of us, following Christ *must* lead to the kind
of life others can likewise follow. We must each make
sure the "epistle" of our lives, read by all men, is one
worth reading.

*"The example of the godly man is a living, standing
memento to all around him of Christ, death and eternity."*
—Cornelius Tyree

TAKE NO THOUGHT

Take therefore no thought for the morrow: for the morrow shall take thought for the things of itself. Sufficient unto the day is the evil thereof (MATTHEW 6:34).

One of the clearest indications the enemy of our souls is at work is when we're thinking of the future and we hear the enemy whisper *What if...* followed by worry-inducing scenarios that shake our faith. Such scenarios as, *What if* there's a food shortage? *What if* there's another pandemic? *What if* there's an atomic war? *What if* Christians are sent to jail? *What if* I lose my job? *What if* my wife leaves? *What if* my child turns away from the Lord?

The list is endless. *Endless!*

But the good news is that our resources in God are also endless. Beyond endless. There is simply no way God's going to run low on anything we need. As for what happens in the future, God is already there. He will not be surprised at world events or at the events that will shape our individual futures.

So as Christian men, we must stand firm against every whispered "What if" and answer it with "God's got this!"

"Worry is the cross which we make for ourselves by over-anxiety." —FRANÇOIS FÉNELON

OVERCOMING THE PAST

Remember ye not the former things, neither consider the things of old. Behold, I will do a new thing; now it shall spring forth; shall ye not know it? I will even make a way in the wilderness, and rivers in the desert (ISAIAH 43:18-19).

What man does not have events in his past he regrets? However, if a man is remembering past sins that God has Himself forgotten because of the forgiveness we find in Christ, those memories are at best wasteful and at worst destructive.

Many a man has labored for years without success to overcome memories of a sinful past. And needlessly so. Every man must acknowledge his past failures and then *move on*. In so doing, God is enabled to open a way through that past wilderness and bring forth rivers in that forsaken desert.

What events of your past still haunt you? Confess them, acknowledge God's forgiveness, and then forevermore, let those memories become monuments to God's mercy and grace.

"Being in Christ, it is safe to forget the past; it is possible to be sure of the future; it is possible to be diligent in the present."
—ALEXANDER MACLAREN

THE COMPLETE MAN

Ye are complete in him, which is the head of all principality and power (COLOSSIANS 2:10).

Aman is incomplete without Christ, but when that man is born again and has become a new creation in Christ, he is reckoned by God as "complete in him."

The full import of that truth may take years to fully appreciate. In fact, many Christian men wander through life for years still feeling incomplete. Recognizing the many benefits of Christ's redemption will clearly continue for as long as a man lives and is worth a lifetime of pondering and appreciating. While many men may strive for a sense of completeness, from God's point of view, a man is already complete when he is "in Christ." What many men assume as a goal, God sees as a starting point.

"Let us understand, that all who have really fled for mercy to the Lord Jesus Christ are, as Paul assures the Colossians, complete in Him! In themselves they may be poor shortcoming sinners—but seeing they have laid hold on Christ, God looks upon them as complete—completely pardoned, completely righteous, completely pure—no jot or tittle of condemnation can be laid to their charge." —J.C. RYLE

WE ARE WARRIORS

Though we walk in the flesh, we do not war after the flesh: (For the weapons of our warfare are not carnal, but mighty through God to the pulling down of strong holds) (2 CORINTHIANS 10:3-4).

Many men, when they were boys, often pretended to be great warriors, fighting for the triumph of good over evil. Now as men, that game of pretense has become reality in that we are all called to be spiritual warriors, not wielding "carnal" weapons, but pulling down satanic strongholds wielding "mighty" spiritual weapons. Praying men are in the front lines of battle today. But they must not battle alone. Every Christian man must join them, equipped for spiritual battle. Passive warriors are an oxymoron.

Today God is calling for men to see the battles for their families, their countries, and their faith for what it is—a tremendous assault from a ruthless enemy. The spiritual army God is assembling is not a volunteer army, it's an army of conscripted men. To be saved is to be enlisted.

"You must watch, pray, and fight. Expect your last battle to be the most difficult, for the enemy's fiercest charge is reserved for the end of the day." —CHARLES SPURGEON

Seasons

To every thing there is a season, and a time to every purpose under the heaven: A time to be born, and a time to die (ECCLESIASTES 3:1-2).

What season of life are you in now? Every man goes through changes as he ages that are, for the most part, God-ordained. Young men are called to bear yokes older men can no longer support. Older men bring wisdom to the table many young men lack.

Happy is the man who is content with whatever season of life he's in. Bitter is the man who laments the passing of one season to the next. God has called us to live the allotted years He's assigned us. We must never look back to a previous season with regret, nor should we look ahead to the next season with presumption. While we are alive today, let's love this present season and fully embrace the gift of life while we can.

"God's purposes have all their seasons of fulfillment. His judgments each have their time of visitation. Mapped out in clear perspective, your every dispensation was fixed from everlasting in the eternal mind of God." —GEORGE MYLNE

A MAN WHO WILL NOT FEAR

God is our refuge and strength, a very present help in trouble. Therefore will not we fear, though the earth be removed, and though the mountains be carried into the midst of the sea; though the waters thereof roar and be troubled, though the mountains shake with the swelling thereof. Selah (PSALM 46:1-3).

E very man is prone to some sort of fear. He may fear financial lack, relationship failure, vocational loss, health decline, and more. But every one of those fears and all others are vanquished when God is our very present help in trouble. Nothing can shake the man whose life is rooted in the providence of God.

When a man is easily shaken, it's time to become *un*shakeable. It's time to shift our burden from our shoulders to God's strong back.

A man's fears may be few or many, but every one of them is conquerable through Christ. The very purpose of trouble in our lives may be God's way of proving Himself as trustworthy while also making us unshakeable.

"God incarnate is the end of fear; and the heart that realizes that He is in the midst...will be quiet in the middle of alarm."
—F.B. MEYER

The Gift of Sex

Flee fornication. Every sin that a man doeth is without the body; but he that committeth fornication sinneth against his own body (1 Corinthians 6:18).

We live in an age when sex as God meant it to be has been greatly diminished. Sexual pleasure is a gift of God to be treasured between a man and his lifetime mate. And yet this gift has been corrupted by Satan to the extent that sexual immorality has been normalized to a staggering degree. Even Christian men are taken in by the promises of porn or the acceptance of sexual sins that were once easily understood as not allowable for men who claim Christ as Lord.

Today, men must flee fornication—in practice and also as entertainment fare in the form of movies and television where sexual permissiveness is routine.

God can restore the rightful place of sexuality in a man's life—if he will renounce any known sexual sin.

The irony is that the gift of sex is enhanced by submitting our desires to God's provision instead of taking the shortcut of sexual sin.

"All sin, particularly the habitual practice of sexual sin, is an unholy boldness in evil!" —Charles Spurgeon

HEROES

And what shall I more say? for the time would fail me to tell of Gedeon, and of Barak, and of Samson, and of Jephthae; of David also, and Samuel, and of the prophets: Who through faith subdued kingdoms, wrought righteousness, obtained promises, stopped the mouths of lions. Quenched the violence of fire, escaped the edge of the sword, out of weakness were made strong, waxed valiant in fight, turned to flight the armies of the aliens (HEBREWS 11:32-34).

Every man needs heroes. Even as boys we looked up to certain men as those we would like to emulate. Heroes abound in the Bible, but who are our heroes of the faith beyond the covers of our Bibles? Have we read the lives of stalwart men like Jim Elliot, Oswald Chambers, Watchman Nee, Ben Carson, and others? Do our children or grandchildren know these men?

May God let us be the best version of the heroes God sees in us. May the heroics of past men of faith show us the way.

"God is preparing His heroes. And when the opportunity comes, He can fit them into their places in a moment. And the world will wonder where they came from." —A.B. SIMPSON

GOD'S WORD

The word of God is quick, and powerful, and sharper than any twoedged sword, piercing even to the dividing asunder of soul and spirit, and of the joints and marrow, and is a discerner of the thoughts and intents of the heart (HEBREWS 4:12).

All scripture is given by inspiration of God, and is profitable for doctrine, for reproof, for correction, for instruction in righteousness (2 TIMOTHY 3:16).

The grass withereth, the flower fadeth: but the word of our God shall stand for ever (ISAIAH 40:8).

When walking in the dark—in our case a dark world—a light is necessary, not optional. Our light is the Word of God. The Word directs us and it corrects us.

Frequent are the temptations to decide for ourselves the right path to take, but without the light of Scripture shining on the path ahead, we're prone to straying from God's will for us. Never make a decision in opposition to God's Word, realizing that such tempting "opportunities" will surely come. Knowing God's Word will save us from many a fall.

"The vigor of our spiritual life will be in exact proportion to the place held by the Bible in our life and thoughts." —GEORGE MÜLLER

RICHES IN HEAVEN

Lay not up for yourselves treasures upon earth, where moth and rust doth corrupt, and where thieves break through and steal: But lay up for yourselves treasures in heaven, where neither moth nor rust doth corrupt, and where thieves do not break through nor steal: For where your treasure is, there will your heart be also (MATTHEW 6:19-21).

Every man must know where his true treasure is…for that's where his heart will follow. The call of God is to reject this earth's riches in favor of incorruptible heavenly treasures.

We work for monetary wages, but the treasures awaiting us in heaven are those we give freely to others in the way of time, love, affirmations, and yes, finances. There is no wiser financial investment than that of giving to others who need what we have. In giving, we find a curious freedom that releases us from the need to gather more into larger barns.

"God's purpose in promising to reward with heavenly and eternal honors the faithful service of His saints is to win them from the pursuit of earthly riches and pleasures, to sustain them in the fires of persecution, and to encourage them in the exercise of Christian virtues." —C.I. SCOFIELD

THE INTEGRITY OF A
CHRISTIAN MAN

The integrity of the upright shall guide them: but the perverseness of transgressors shall destroy them (PROVERBS 11:3).

There is a reward to the man of integrity that money can't buy. Likewise, there is a perversity to dishonest men that will soon destroy them. A Christian man knows by God's Word and by experience that in the long run (and often in the short run), honesty and integrity pay good dividends.

Integrity can be learned in the same way anything can be learned—and that's by experience. Hang with other men of integrity and follow their example. Remember to always choose the right thing, even when it's hard to do so. Eventually, choosing the right thing will become your default action.

"Be satisfied and thankful, you who are taught by the Spirit of God, to walk in integrity. You are rich in faith, and heirs of the kingdom—and in this world you have and shall have everything that infinite wisdom and divine love sees fit for you!" —GEORGE LAWSON

Working as unto God

Whatsoever ye do, do it heartily, as to the Lord, and not unto men; knowing that of the Lord ye shall receive the reward of the inheritance: for ye serve the Lord Christ (Colossians 3:23-24).

Every man has a calling. For some, it's a calling based on a secular career. Others may have a calling based on talent. For others, the calling is based on a learned ability. Yet others may work in full-time ministry. But no matter what our calling—from plumber to salesman to executive to pastor—we are not working for another person. Our work is first, last, and always unto God.

Excellence in our calling is mandatory. And though we may fail many times, we still pursue the goal of the "reward of the inheritance" reserved for those who have worked "as to the Lord."

"No duty should be done with half a heart, or half a hand. Let not the heart be absent while the hand is at work...Seek the way of working quietly with sober diligence and peaceful energy; and thus whatever you do, you will do it with all your might." —George Mylne

God's Sovereignty

*Declaring the end from the beginning, and from ancient
times the things that are not yet done, saying, My counsel
shall stand, and I will do all my pleasure* (Isaiah 46:10).

During the course of a lifetime, a man enjoys much
and suffers much. During the former, we rejoice at
the graciousness of God, but do we also trust in God during the latter times?

Yes, we do, if we understand that the purposes of
God shall always stand, regardless of man's opinion—
and that those purposes always work toward a goal God
has in mind.

Trust in God's sovereignty lifts a huge burden from
our backs. And instead of paralyzing our prayer life
("Why pray if God has predetermined the outcome?"),
it invigorates our prayers. In praying, we participate in
God bringing about His sovereignty.

Prayer has been likened to laying down the railroad
tracks where the locomotive of God's will wants to go.
Pray then with confidence and expectation.

*"Divine sovereignty is not the sovereignty of a tyrannical Despot, but the exercised pleasure of One who is infinitely wise
and good! Because God is infinitely wise He cannot err, and
because He is infinitely righteous He will not do wrong."*
—A.W. Pink

The Joy of the Lord

O come, let us sing unto the LORD: let us make a joyful noise to the rock of our salvation. Let us come before his presence with thanksgiving, and make a joyful noise unto him with psalms. For the LORD is a great God, and a great King above all gods (PSALM 95:1-3).

A joyless Christian is an oxymoron. There's no lack of joy to be found in Christianity. As we learn to live in the joy of the Lord, we find renewed strength during hard times. We find happiness during blessed times.

Christian joy is not a worked-up emotion. It comes as a gift from the Lord Himself. In *Him* is fullness of joy. The package deal of salvation contains more than enough joy to meet life's demands. Therefore, come before His presence with thanksgiving, and make a joyful noise with psalms.

Why? Because He "is a great God and a great King above all gods."

"There exists a delight that is not given to the wicked, but to those honoring Thee, O God, without desiring recompense, the joy of whom Thou art Thyself! And this is the blessed life, to rejoice towards Thee, about Thee, for Thy sake."
—AUGUSTINE

A Man's Body

Know ye not that your body is the temple of the Holy Ghost which is in you, which ye have of God, and ye are not your own? (1 CORINTHIANS 6:19).

No man ever yet hated his own flesh; but nourisheth and cherisheth it, even as the Lord the church (EPHESIANS 5:29).

When we came to Christ in faith, along came our bodies. We surrendered all to Him, body, soul, and spirit. Our bodies that were once Pizza Huts are now God's temple.

In the past we may have been less than kind to our temples, but it's never too late to refurbish a weathered structure. Treat your body with respect. Eat right, get some exercise, sleep well, and maintain a positive attitude. Our body is one of God's great gifts.

"It is the part of a Christian to take care of his own body for the very purpose that by its soundness and well-being he may be enabled to labor for the aid of those who are in want, and thus the stronger member may serve the weaker member."
—MARTIN LUTHER

God's Call on Your Life

Who hath saved us, and called us with an holy calling, not according to our works, but according to his own purpose and grace, which was given us in Christ Jesus before the world began (2 Timothy 1:9).

As our years pass, it may be hard to remember the call God has on our lives. Despite our busyness, there are prayers to be prayed, work to be done, hungry to be fed, young Christians to be taught. There is always work to be done in God's kingdom, and every man has his place of service.

It's up to each man to step up to the plate and fulfill his calling from God. When we're unsure of God's calling, we can pray, we can ask others what they see as God's calling in us, and we can simply begin filling needs we notice around us. The years will still pass, but like a bank account with compound interest, the work of God continues onward, building up God's house.

"Worldliness is a spirit, a temperament, an attitude of the soul. It is a life without high callings, life devoid of lofty ideals. It is a gaze always horizontal and never vertical." —John Jowett

THE HOLY GHOST

Now the God of hope fill you with all joy and peace in believing, that ye may abound in hope, through the power of the Holy Ghost (ROMANS 15:13).

There is no Christian life apart from a relationship with each member of the Trinity. We come to know God as our Father, Jesus Christ as Savior, and the Holy Ghost as comforter, teacher, helper, and guide.

Many men know God as their father and Jesus as their Savior but may be shaky when it comes to the Holy Ghost. And yet, in God's plan, our power for living comes from this third member of the Godhead. Never underestimate the privilege of a relationship with the Holy Ghost, for He brings joy, boldness, and guidance for living.

"If there be one God subsisting in three persons, then let us give equal reverence to all the persons in the Trinity. There is not more or less in the Trinity; the Father is not more God than the Son and Holy Ghost. There is an order in the Godhead, but no degrees; one person has not a majority or super eminence above another, therefore we must give equal worship to all the persons." —THOMAS WATSON

THE PRAYING CHRISTIAN MAN

Verily I say unto you, If ye have faith, and doubt not, ye shall not only do this which is done to the fig tree, but also if ye shall say unto this mountain, Be thou removed, and be thou cast into the sea; it shall be done. And all things, whatsoever ye shall ask in prayer, believing, ye shall receive (MATTHEW 21:21-22).

A Christian man is a praying man. Prayer is the essential tool of the Christian life. Not only is it our means of communing with our Lord, but prayer is the means by which God has chosen to attend to our needs.

The Bible is chock-full of answered prayers. The people of God repeatedly prayed for deliverance from enemies and were saved. Barren women prayed for children and became mothers. Sinners prayed for forgiveness and became men who changed not only the course of their lives but the course of history.

Sadly, many men pray far too little. But if we could realize the power of a praying man—we would fall to our knees more often.

Pray much. Believe much. Move mountains.

"The story of every great Christian achievement is the history of answered prayer."—E.M. BOUNDS

ALL FOR CHRIST

Then one of them, which was a lawyer, asked him a question, tempting him, and saying, Master, which is the great commandment in the law? Jesus said unto him, Thou shalt love the Lord thy God with all thy heart, and with all thy soul, and with all thy mind (MATTHEW 22:35-37).

There's no such thing as a partial Christian. A man either is or is not a Christian. The requirement is to love God with all one's heart, soul, and mind and to seek first the kingdom of God. This is total commitment. It means all a man does, plans, or desires is related to God's plan for that man. We must often ask ourselves, Are we seeking God first, trusting all else will be added to us?

"May not a single moment of my life be spent outside the light, love and joy of God's presence and not a moment without the entire surrender of myself as a vessel for Him to fill full of His Spirit and His love." —ANDREW MURRAY

The Love of God

Behold, what manner of love the Father hath bestowed upon us, that we should be called the sons of God (1 John 3:1).

The contemplation of God's love for us can change us. As we "behold" the manner of God's love, we realize it far surpasses human love. God saw us before time began. He saw to our conceptions, our births, and oversees every day of our lives—and then His love ushers us into eternal existence with Him. There is nothing about God's love for us that can leave us in want. When we are consumed by this divine love God has for each of us, we need have no fear, no worry—and we are able to forgive and truly love others, even our enemies.

"Behold, what manner of love is this, that Christ should be arraigned and we adorned, that the curse should be laid on His head and the crown set on ours." —Thomas Watson

The Favor of God

Thou, LORD, wilt bless the righteous; with favor wilt thou compass him as with a shield (PSALM 5:12).

The lines are fallen unto me in pleasant places; yea, I have a goodly heritage (PSALM 16:6).

It's no small thing to acknowledge the blessing of God on the righteous man. Our heavenly Father delights to bring blessing to His children. He also bestows favor on the Christian man, sometimes openly and sometimes in secret.

A man who is benefitting from God's favor may never really know how God worked His plan behind the scenes to bring about a desired end. Even now, God has blessings for you, and He bestows favor on you. This is the heritage of those who trust in God and are busy in His vineyard. The lines fall in pleasant places for you.

"The devil visits idle men with his temptations. God visits industrious men with His favors." —MATTHEW HENRY

God's Promises for a Man

The promise is unto you, and to your children, and to all that are afar off, even as many as the Lord our God shall call (ACTS 2:39).

The promise of God—indeed all the promises of God—are for those of us who are "afar off" from when Luke wrote the book of Acts. The godly man prospers as he searches the Bible for the appropriate promises that relate to his life and his trials. The unprepared man who knows little of God's promises may find himself adrift without an anchor in times of trouble and uncertainty.

What promises of God will you bring to bear today on your present need? Read them, repeat them, believe them.

"Furnish thyself with arguments from the promises to enforce thy prayers, and make them prevalent with God. The promises are the ground of faith, and faith, when strengthened, will make thee fervent, and such fervency ever speeds and returns with victory out of the field of prayer. The mightier any is in the Word, the more mighty he will be in prayer."
—WILLIAM GURNALL

Let God Choose

He shall subdue the people under us, and the nations under our feet. He shall choose our inheritance for us, the excellency of Jacob whom he loved. Selah (PSALM 47:3-4).

Many Christian men have made the discovery that God knows far better than they do how to choose among life's decisions. Our human way of choosing is often at variance with God's way.

We know for certain that a decision that in some way violates God's Word is a wrong decision. Many men have also discovered that when God chooses, He often doesn't work on our timetable. The Bible is full of cautions to "wait on the Lord." Waiting is hard, but if we are to reap God's superior choice, it will be worth it. We must not get ahead of God, but neither must we lag behind. Pray, wait in faith, and see what God chooses for you. It will be a sweet "inheritance."

"The sweetest lesson I have learned in God's school is to let the Lord choose for me." —D.L. MOODY

GODLY PROSPERITY

Blessed is the man that walketh not in the counsel of the ungodly, nor standeth in the way of sinners, nor sitteth in the seat of the scornful...he shall be like a tree planted by the rivers of water, that bringeth forth his fruit in his season; his leaf also shall not wither; and whatsoever he doeth shall prosper (PSALM 1:1,3).

God never desires for a man to fail at life. Instead, God offers every man a way to succeed, though that success may not duplicate what the world calls success.

If a man doesn't walk in the counsel of the ungodly (the world), nor live sinfully, nor scorn God's ways, that man can reckon himself a fruitful tree planted by rivers of water.

Be cautioned though. Never expect your prosperity to be accepted as such by those who measure prosperity with the wrong gauge.

"There are great positives as well as refusals necessary for him who would find real prosperity. He must not only say no to the wrong, he must say yes to the right. He must not only avoid the seat of the scornful, but his delight must be in the law of the Lord." —CLOVIS CHAPPELL

THE RETURN OF CHRIST

Ye men of Galilee, why stand ye gazing up into heaven? this same Jesus, which is taken up from you into heaven, shall so come in like manner as ye have seen him go into heaven (ACTS 1:11).

Looking for that blessed hope, and the glorious appearing of the great God and our Savior Jesus Christ (TITUS 2:13).

Christian men differ on the timeline of Christ's return, but most do look forward to that "blessed hope" with anticipation. Every generation has this hope and sees clear signs that the great day will soon arrive. The return of Christ holds significant meaning for every Christian man. It's an incentive to live a pure, unstained life in the midst of a crooked generation. It's a guard against fear as troubling world events unfold, and it's a motive to support worldwide evangelism—and personal evangelism too. With this blessed hope within us, we must be prepared to share with others the source of our hope.

"When He returns is not as important as the fact that we are ready for Him when He does return." —A.W. TOZER

UNIQUELY YOU

O Lord, thou hast searched me, and known me. Thou knowest my downsitting and mine uprising, thou understandest my thought afar off. Thou compassest my path and my lying down, and art acquainted with all my ways. For there is not a word in my tongue, but, lo, O LORD, thou knowest it altogether. Thou hast beset me behind and before, and laid thine hand upon me. Such knowledge is too wonderful for me; it is high, I cannot attain unto it (PSALM 139:1-6).

The imprint of God is upon every Christian man. God designed us in His image. He prepared a plan for us in order to have a blessed life. God knows our very thoughts before we think them. He knows the next words out of our mouths. He is acquainted with all our ways.

Such knowledge must change us—and for the better. Our God is, of all things, an intimate God. We can be who we are with Him because He knows us better than we know ourselves. Comprehending God's intimacy in our lives is too wonderful to grasp…and yet it is so.

"You are the only you God made…God made you and broke the mold." —MAX LUCADO

WAITING ON GOD

Wait on the LORD: be of good courage, and he shall strengthen thine heart: wait, I say, on the LORD (PSALM 27:14).

Few men enjoy waiting on God. Truth be told, if we ran things, we would be far hastier than we judge God to be. And we'd be all the poorer for it. We may think we need our answer *now,* but God knows the exact timing to bring our lives' plans to pass.

As we wait, we must remember we're not waiting passively. We're waiting with anticipation, knowing God *will* bring to pass that needful event. He asks only that we be of good courage, and He shall strengthen our hearts. Whatever it is you're waiting to hear from God, pray with expectancy, and it shall come to pass in His time and in His way.

"The prayer that begins with trustfulness, and passes on into waiting, will always end in thankfulness, triumph, and praise." —ALEXANDER MACLAREN

By the Grace of God

The grace of our Lord was exceeding abundant with faith and love which is in Christ Jesus (1 Timothy 1:14).

We often sing of God's "amazing grace," but do we stop to think that part of our amazement is at the depth of God's grace toward us? It's not that His grace barely saves us; no, it's that His grace *abundantly* saves us. And having saved us, His grace follows us through life to our dying day. The supply simply never runs dry. It never will. It cannot. God's grace sustains us with every word we speak, every step we take, every thought we think.

On the following page, you'll find all the verses to the most sung hymn of all time. Take a few moments to read and ponder each stanza. Experience afresh the amazing grace of our God.

"Through many dangers, toils and snares, I have already come; 'Tis grace hath brought me safe thus far, And grace will lead me home." —John Newton

Amazing Grace

Amazing grace! How sweet the sound
that saved a wretch like me!
I once was lost, but now am found;
was blind, but now I see.

'Twas grace that taught my heart to fear,
and grace my fears relieved;
How precious did that grace appear
the hour I first believed.

Through many dangers, toils and snares,
I have already come;
'Tis grace hath brought me safe thus far,
and grace will lead me home.

The Lord has promised good to me,
His Word my hope secures;
He will my Shield and Portion be,
as long as life endures.

Yea, when this flesh and heart shall fail,
and mortal life shall cease,
I shall possess, within the veil,
a life of joy and peace.

When we've been there ten thousand years,
bright shining as the sun,
We've no less days to sing God's praise
than when we'd first begun.

GOD'S PRESENCE

Thou wilt show me the path of life: in thy presence is fulness of joy; at thy right hand there are pleasures for evermore (PSALM 16:11).

A Christian man is never without the presence of God. Our Lord surrounds us moment by moment; we are never out of His care.

And in His presence, what do we find? We discover "fulness of joy." What do we *not* find in His presence? We do not find anger (having made peace with God through the Cross), we do not find fear (for He has told us time after time to "fear not"). We find no hatred (save the hatred of sin). We find no burden (for He bears our burdens for us).

"Fulness of joy," indeed! And pleasures forevermore!

"We should go into His presence as a child goes to his father. We do it with reverence and godly fear, of course, but we should go with a childlike confidence and simplicity." —MARTYN LLOYD-JONES

Time

Whereas ye know not what shall be on the morrow. For what is your life? It is even a vapor, that appeareth for a little time, and then vanisheth away (JAMES 4:14).

What a precious gift is time! Hours, weeks, months, and years in which we live and thrive in the presence of God. We live by the power of the Holy Spirit, moment by moment. Every second we breathe is accounted for by God—and is given to us as a gift to enjoy but also as a charge to act as stewards. How then can we best allot our time on earth so as to maximize our usefulness? James has the right idea when he reminds us our lives are but vapors. He says we do not know what will happen tomorrow. The implication is that we have only today to be sure of, so if we will use our time wisely, we will use it *today*. A useful day includes prayer, taking in God's Word, obedience to anything we know we must do today, and trusting in guidance from the Holy Spirit. If we fill our days thus, we will arrive at life's end with contentment. Even if that day is tomorrow.

"O God, impress upon me the value of time, and give regulation to all my thoughts and to all my movements."—THOMAS CHALMERS

A Man's Good Memories

The memory of the just is blessed: but the name of the wicked shall rot (PROVERBS 10:7).

As we move through life, we are accumulating memories. For many, those memories may consist of failure, sin, and missed opportunities. But to dwell on those past failures does us no good. We must always remember to put *all* our sins and missteps of the past under the blood of Christ. The recalling of a painful past is only of use to our enemy, Satan, who will continue to accuse us as long as we allow him to do so—even for years. God, on the other hand, would have us cleanse our memories of that regretted past and dwell on memories of His faithfulness.

What is past is simply what He has brought us through and now can only be recalled as a monument to His goodness. Store up your godly memories. Discard forever the memories that stab you afresh with each recollection.

"Gratitude changes the pangs of memory into a tranquil joy."
—DIETRICH BONHOEFFER

MIRACLES

He that believeth on me, the works that I do shall he do also;
and greater works than these shall he do; because I go unto my
Father. And whatsoever ye shall ask in my name, that will I do,
that the Father may be glorified in the Son (JOHN 14:12-13).

Do miracles still happen? Do you need a miracle? I
suspect all Christian men need a miracle at various times. We have God's promise of provision throughout our lives even when that provision requires a miracle. But we must remember that not all miracles are instantaneous. God works fast miracles, and He works slow miracles. If you need a miracle, pray for it. Then wait and see how God brings it about without your dictating how it must be performed. Trust is always the key to experiencing a miracle.

"Have you been asking God what He is going to do? He will
never tell you. God does not tell you what He is going to do,
He reveals to you who He is. Do you believe in a miracle work-
ing God, and will you 'go out' in complete surrender to Him
until you are not surprised one iota by anything He does?"
—OSWALD CHAMBERS

THE WIDE-OPEN
DOOR OF MERCY

Mercy unto you, and peace, and love, be multiplied (JUDE 1:2).

The matter of sin—perhaps ongoing sin—must be dealt with severely in the man who desires to rise up before God. Sin in a Christian man can delay the work of God in our lives. Yes, the door of mercy remains open if we sin, but our days of ongoing sinful selfish living must be considered as behind us.

If there is sin, we need only apply God's remedy: repentance, confession, and an understanding that Christ has paid for *all* our sin. We need never wallow in the sad aftermath of sin. Once sin is repented of and confessed, the Christian man has only to rise up as a ransomed man and walk confidently forward, enjoying the mercies of God.

Is there any sin you have yet to deal with? Don't delay. Don't allow sin to hold you back from your destiny any longer.

"Every ransomed man owes his salvation to the fact that during his days of sinning, God kept the door of mercy open by refusing to accept any of his evil acts as final." —A. W. TOZER

CHRIST IN US

I am crucified with Christ: nevertheless I live; yet not I, but Christ liveth in me: and the life which I now live in the flesh I live by the faith of the Son of God, who loved me, and gave himself for me (GALATIANS 2:20).

There is a secret to living the Christian life, though it's really not so secret, since God has revealed it to us in His Word. That secret is to see ourselves—our old fallen lives—as crucified with Christ. And though we live on, we do so by Christ living in us and through us.

This is no abstract symbolism. This is God's reality for the Christian. We die to self in order to find true life in Christ. We die; He lives in us.

How is this accomplished? As all God's truth is accomplished in the believer—by faith.

Classic books have revealed this secret in more depth. One of the best is *Hudson Taylor's Spiritual Secret* by Dr. and Mrs. Howard Taylor.

"Christ liveth in me. And how great the difference…instead of bondage, liberty; instead of failure, quiet victories within; instead of fear and weakness, a restful sense of sufficiency in Another." —HUDSON TAYLOR

BE GLAD AND LAUGH

A merry heart doeth good like a medicine: but a broken spirit drieth the bones (PROVERBS 17:22).

Our present world has much that rends our hearts and can bring tears to the manliest of men. But amid the pain of a suffering world, there are men to be found who remember how to have a joyful heart—how to laugh despite adversity. God is looking for more men who are willing to be dispensers of heavenly joy in an often hellish world. We're told in Ecclesiastes 3:4 that there's a time to weep…but also a time to laugh.

A godly man knows the difference between the two. When his friend is in pain, he will weep with him. But when a joyful heart is the prescribed medicine, the Christian brings the joy of the Lord to bear on the situation.

Today, may your life bring you something about which you can laugh. Even in a tough situation…find joy. This too shall pass.

"Be glad and laugh from the low bottom of thine own heart."
—WILLIAM TYNDALE

LOVE NOT THE WORLD

Love not the world, neither the things that are in the world. If any man love the world, the love of the Father is not in him (1 JOHN 2:15).

Every Christian man has his weaknesses when it comes to "the world." At every turn we're tempted to love the things of this world. And one man's worldly temptation is easily discounted by another man who has his own worldly battles.

But to love the world is to *not* love the Father. Our hearts must not be divided. We give our allegiance to God and count the world as God's enemy.

After having been burned by flirtations with the world, many men come to realize this world is simply a place to pass through on our way to eternity. For sure, God gives us pleasures in this life, but they are pleasures of His choosing, not of our own fleshly appetites.

Though we are *in* the world, we are not of the world, which will eventually—with all its attractions—dissolve in flames.

"Christianity removes the attraction of the earth; and this is one way in which it diminishes men's burden. It makes them citizens of another world." —HENRY DRUMMOND

KINGDOM LIVING

As ye know how we exhorted and comforted and charged every one of you, as a father doth his children, that ye would walk worthy of God, who hath called you unto his kingdom and glory (1 THESSALONIANS 2:11-12).

A Christian man is a kingdom man. He has been uprooted from this present world and replanted in God's kingdom. Forever after his conversion, his life is lived as one who is becoming more and more acquainted and comfortable as a resident of God's kingdom—a kingdom to which we were called. A kingdom for which we were each personally chosen by God.

Learning kingdom living is a man's greatest joy on earth, influencing all he does. For that reason, we must walk worthy of God, eternally grateful for our place in His kingdom.

"I will place no value on anything I have or may possess except in relation to the kingdom of Christ." —DAVID LIVINGSTONE

Rest

Come unto me, all ye that labor and are heavy laden, and I will give you rest. Take my yoke upon you, and learn of me; for I am meek and lowly in heart: and ye shall find rest unto your souls. For my yoke is easy, and my burden is light (Matthew 11:28-30).

Is there any burden a man can have that's beyond the power of Christ to bear? No, there is not. He bids us take up His easy yoke. He invites us to find rest for our souls. No matter how heavy *our* burdens, His is light.

Every day we're invited to enter a burden-free day, trusting all to Him.

Have you laid down today's burden? Have you taken up His light load? Have you found rest for your soul? His offer is to "come unto me." It's an offer no burdened man should refuse.

"Abide in Me says Jesus. Cling to Me. Stick fast to Me. Live the life of close and intimate communion with Me. Get nearer to Me. Roll every burden on Me. Cast your whole weight on Me. Never let go your hold on Me for a moment…Do this and I will never fail you." —J.C. Ryle

REDEEMED BY THE BLOOD

Forasmuch as ye know that ye were not redeemed with corruptible things, as silver and gold, from your vain conversation received by tradition from your fathers; but with the precious blood of Christ, as of a lamb without blemish and without spot (1 PETER 1:18-19).

Throughout the Bible, blood is a means of salvation. We read this in the Passover story where the blood of an innocent lamb was the means of escaping the angel of death. It was a foreshadowing of the true Lamb of God, Christ who saves us from the penalty for our sins.

For many people, the blood of Christ is a topic to avoid. And yet the blood of Christ is central to our salvation. Never disparage the bloody sacrifice on the Cross. Never apologize for claiming the blood. Ponder the irony of the innocent Lamb dying to save the guilty. The Lamb who suffers death so we may live.

Yes, the blood is that important.

"I am ready to meet God face to face tonight and look into those eyes of infinite holiness, for all my sins are covered by the atoning blood." —R.A. TORREY

FIRSTFRUITS

Honor the LORD with thy substance, and with the firstfruits of all thine increase: So shall thy barns be filled with plenty, and thy presses shall burst out with new wine (PROVERBS 3:9-10).

Christian men are givers. We give to the poor, to the church, but above all, we give to God. And not just what's left over at the end of the month. No, we give from the firstfruits of our labors. We give God from the best of the crop before we take for ourselves. Besides money, our giving includes our time, attention, talents… whatever the need, if we can fill it, we're there.

Whether the giving is of ourselves or our finances, it should be at the forefront of our offering. Leftovers are not good enough for the Lord. Every man must consider *how* God can best use him and his resources. What among our "firstfruits" are we able to give generously and without regret?

"God, who is the first and best, must have the first and best of everything; his right is prior to all other, and therefore he must be served first." —MATTHEW HENRY

THE FEAR OF THE LORD

The fear of the LORD is the beginning of knowledge: but fools despise wisdom and instruction (PROVERBS 1:7).

The fear of the LORD is to hate evil: pride, and arrogancy, and the evil way, and the froward mouth, do I hate (PROVERBS 8:13).

It has been rightly said that the fear of the Lord is the fear that banishes all other fears. But even more, the fear of God is the beginning of knowledge and wisdom. On the reverse side, fearing God means to hate evil, pride, and arrogance.

When the fear of God is absent in a man's life, he loses out on the knowledge and wisdom God has provided for him. Likewise, an acceptance of evil and pride in a man's life not only shows a lack of godly fear; it also opens the door to unwise choices and destructive behavior.

Fearing God gives a man a right reason to rejoice, for it's then he knows he's protected by his wisdom and able to avoid Satan's evil traps set for his destruction.

"The fear of God is the cornerstone of all blessedness. We must reverence the ever-blessed God, before we can be blessed ourselves." —CHARLES SPURGEON

ADVERSITY

If thou faint in the day of adversity, thy strength is small (PROVERBS 24:10).

There are times in a man's life when he faces adversity. It could be a broken relationship, a health crisis, financial loss, or some other tragedy. At such times a man's faith is tested. Will he make it through the trial unscathed and wiser for the experience, or will his faith suffer under the weight of adversity? During good times a man will find it easy to rejoice in God's goodness. But can he also rejoice as he walks through the deep weeds of life?

No matter where you are today, rejoice. If all is well, be grateful. If under the cloud of adversity, let the experience enlarge your trust in God. Every trial has its eventual resolution. Let God lead the way to that end.

"Adversity is not simply a tool. It's God's most effective tool for the advancement of our spiritual lives. The circumstances and events we see as setbacks are oftentimes the very things that launch us into periods of intense spiritual growth. Once we begin to understand this, and accept it as a spiritual fact of life, adversity becomes easier to bear." —CHARLES STANLEY

Peace with God

Being justified by faith, we have peace with God through our Lord Jesus Christ (Romans 5:1).

In a world that doesn't know peace—real peace—it's all the more important for Christian men to model the peace available to all through Christ. How is it we have this supernatural peace? It's because we're justified by faith. That means God does not count our sins against us. Our records are clean. Expunged. No guilt. No reason to live under the weight of an uneasy conscience.

Every day we freely have this peace. It's not a temporary truce with an adversary with the potential for future skirmishes to resume. No, this peace is ours for today, tomorrow, and forever. This peace is so good, it's something we must share with others who know no peace.

"If you are not at peace with God—then you are at peace with Satan." —James Smith

A SECURE FUTURE

For I know the thoughts that I think toward you, saith the LORD, *thoughts of peace, and not of evil, to give you an expected end* (JEREMIAH 29:11).

Every man thinks about his future. *Will I be happy? Will I live to a ripe old age? Will my finances last?* All these and more pass through every man's mind. And when that happens, we should think of it as a prompt to reaffirm our trust that God has plans for us that are of peace, to give us an expected end. The road to that end will surely include bumps along the way, but a safe arrival is guaranteed. Even on this very day, God has His plan for you in mind and sees to it that the plan is fully operational, bringing you to the very place God destined you to be.

Confidence in God's ability to bring us to an expected end eliminates worry and needless concern. You have a future with a desired end, designed by God.

"Trust the past to God's mercy, the present to God's love and the future to God's providence." —AUGUSTINE

UNDER THE CIRCUMSTANCES?

For I am persuaded, that neither death, nor life, nor angels, nor principalities, nor powers, nor things present, nor things to come, nor height, nor depth, nor any other creature, shall be able to separate us from the love of God, which is in Christ Jesus our Lord (ROMANS 8:38-39).

When asked how they're doing, some men reply, "Okay, I guess…under the circumstances." But why would we allow ourselves to be *under* a pile of circumstances that render our attitudes as only okay? From God's point of view, we're not to be "under" anything except His care for us.

When you feel circumstances beginning to pile up, take a step back and consider what God would have you do to either change those circumstances or adjust your attitude.

Get on top—stay on top!

"No one can get above circumstances unless he knows that he has the ear of God. The power of intercession is a great thing to the servant of God." —G.V. WIGRAM

The Power of Praise

By him therefore let us offer the sacrifice of praise to God continually, that is, the fruit of our lips giving thanks to his name (HEBREWS 13:15).

I will praise thee, O LORD, with my whole heart; I will show forth all thy marvelous works (PSALM 9:1).

Praising God brings power to the Christian man. And while it's great to develop an attitude of praise, don't let it stop there. Vocalize your praise. If you're alone, perhaps in your car or in your office, speak aloud your praise of God. Let the fruit of your lips give thanks to the God who created you and sustains you. Let your whole heart praise God for His marvelous works. Praise Him not just for what He does in your life, but praise Him simply for who He is.

Throughout the day, busy or not, try to take short praise breaks and find yourself renewed.

"Praise lies upon a higher plain than thanksgiving. When I give thanks, my thoughts still circle around myself to some extent. But in praise my soul ascends to self-forgetting adoration, seeing and praising only the majesty and power of God, His grace and redemption." —OLE HALLESBY

Boundaries

I have set the LORD always before me: because he is at my right hand, I shall not be moved (PSALM 16:8).

Many Christian men find themselves in trouble because they have violated boundaries that were designed to keep them safe.

Boundaries are like guardrails on a mountainous highway. How foolish to skirt the guardrails and hope nothing calamitous happens.

What boundaries are in place for you? What boundaries guard your eyes against pornography? What boundaries guard your mouth? Your feet? If your boundaries are weak, it's time for either a reset or to establish them for the first time. If you already have firm boundaries, hold fast to them. A boundaryless man is on the trail of danger.

"You will often have observed, while walking along some footpath that winds its way amid the fields, a flock of sheep quietly feeding within an enclosure made by portable fences. Instead of roaming the whole field over, they are located on one small spot, until the shepherd shifting the simple fence, makes the furthest boundary the commencement of another plot of feeding ground—and so on, until every portion of the field has, in its turn, yielded food and sweetness to the flock."
—ARCHIBALD BROWN

ADDICTED TO JOY

The joy of the LORD is your strength (NEHEMIAH 8:10).

Addictions have been around for centuries, and always with the same goal—to try to fill the joy-starved centers of our beings. But God has a better solution: find our joy in Him. Allow His joy to be our strength. Of necessity, this means turning from our addictions, turning from all that would enslave us, and accepting the joy that comes from above. This joy fills us, never leaving us unsatisfied. It's a supernatural joy—one that is eternal. In this joy we find treasures far beyond the carnal and momentary pleasures our addictions offer us.

Be done with addictions. Seek only true spiritual joy. Let it be the source of your strength.

"Man cannot live without joy; therefore when he is deprived of true spiritual joys it is necessary that he become addicted to carnal pleasures." —THOMAS AQUINAS

A MAN WHO SERVES

If it seem evil unto you to serve the LORD, choose you this day whom ye will serve (JOSHUA 24:15).

Every man faces the crucial choice of who he will serve. Will it be self, by amassing a fortune, becoming well-known, or indulging in the pleasures of this life? God's alternative is a life dedicated to serving Him and Him alone. The irony is that those who choose the former are faced with often unexpected detours from true happiness.

Serving God, on the other hand, also provides many unexpected detours in life. But God's detours take us by the fountains of joy, the streams of right living, the glories of a reward for a life well-lived.

Every day a man must consciously or unconsciously be living out his choice. Today may offer opportunities to remind yourself of the choice you've made.

"Thanks be to God, there is hope today; this very hour you can choose Him and serve Him." —D. L. MOODY

FULL SURRENDER

My son, give me thine heart, and let thine eyes observe my ways (PROVERBS 23:26).

A man may be a Christian, may even be looked up to as a man of great faith, and yet he alone knows he's kept a part of his heart for himself. Oh, he may not think of it like that, but when pressed by the God who is seeking his whole heart, he will confess to that hidden closet where his secret abides.

God's plea for our hearts isn't just because God is collecting hearts. No, it's because God knows that true happiness and fulfillment are found when a man's entire life—closets and all—are His and His alone.

"Unless you have made a complete surrender and are doing his will it will avail you nothing if you've reformed a thousand times and have your name on fifty church records."
—BILLY SUNDAY

QUICK TO HEAR

My beloved brethren, let every man be swift to hear, slow to speak, slow to wrath (JAMES 1:19).

A man in a race will want to go as fast as he can. A sick man wants to be well *now*. A man seeking wealth will take shortcuts if it will fatten his bank account. But a man of God knows that when it comes to the ears, tongue, and temper, slow is better than fast.

A good man will slow down and listen, not just hear. He will measure his words before speaking. His wrath, if stirred, is subject to a cooling-off period.

God's call to men is to slow down in all aspects of life, but especially in those areas where we rush to judgment, speak unwisely, or make later regrettable decisions.

"God has given us two ears, but one tongue, to show that we should be swift to hear, but slow to speak. God has set a double fence before the tongue, the teeth and the lips, to teach us to be wary that we offend not with our tongue." —THOMAS WATSON

Heaven

Blessed be the God and Father of our Lord Jesus Christ, which according to his abundant mercy hath begotten us again unto a lively hope by the resurrection of Jesus Christ from the dead, to an inheritance incorruptible, and undefiled, and that fadeth not away, reserved in heaven for you, who are kept by the power of God through faith unto salvation ready to be revealed in the last time (1 PETER 1:3-5).

While here on earth, we can only ponder what heaven will be like. We know our heavenly inheritance will be incorruptible, undefiled, and eternal. Until then, we're confident in God's ability to keep us by His power, through our faith. Whatever our thoughts of heaven, they're way too modest. Consider our God and His ability to create. Consider His great love for each of us. Consider an eternity with God and all those who have gone before us.

Ponder heaven today. Take a moment here and there to consider your future abode.

Is it any wonder our hope for heaven is a *lively* hope?

"I wonder many times that ever a child of God should have a sad heart, considering what the Lord is preparing for him."
—SAMUEL RUTHERFORD

ABIDING

Abide in me, and I in you. As the branch cannot bear fruit of itself, except it abide in the vine; no more can ye, except ye abide in me. I am the vine, ye are the branches: He that abideth in me, and I in him, the same bringeth forth much fruit: for without me ye can do nothing (JOHN 15:4-5).

Foolish is the man who thinks he can bear fruit by simply exerting himself. Such fruit, should it exist, isn't fit for consumption. And yet we're commanded to be fruit-bearing Christians, so how is this to be? Clearly, there's only one way—and that's to abide in Christ, just as a branch abides in the vine. It is through Him that we not only bear fruit, but bear *much* fruit. Apart from Christ, we can do nothing.

Today, relax in your connection to the vine. Let there be much fruit that comes from simply abiding.

"We shall never abide in Christ as we ought, unless we hear more of Christ, read more of Christ, and think more of Christ. But we must not stop at thinking, hearing, or reading of Christ—we must actually commune with Christ." —J.R. MILLER

THE STRAIT GATE

Enter ye in at the strait gate: for wide is the gate, and broad is the way, that leadeth to destruction, and many there be which go in thereat (MATTHEW 7:13).

It's astonishing that so many men take the broad way leading to destruction. To do so, they must pass by the narrow gate and either ignore it or miss seeing it entirely.

They have chosen the broad way that seems right. Yet we have chosen the narrow way that leads to life.

Through our journey, we're presented with additional versions of the broad way: the lucrative job offer filled with compromise, the sexually immoral invitation, the purchase of material goods we can't afford.

The Christian life is a continual passing succession of gate after gate until we find the right one—the narrow gate of God's will.

"He that will be knighted must kneel for it, and he that will enter in at the strait gate must crowd for it—a gate made so on purpose, narrow and hard in the entrance, yet, after we have entered, wide and glorious, that after our pain our joy may be the sweeter." —THOMAS ADAMS

THE LIFE OF PRAYER

[Jesus] cometh unto the disciples, and findeth them asleep, and saith unto Peter, What, could ye not watch with me one hour? (MATTHEW 26:40).

The Christian man who rises up for the Lord knows that prayer—diligent prayer—is crucial to fulfilling his calling. The seeds of his ministry—whether large or small—are sown in the prayer closet. Short prayers are welcome. But so are lengthy prayers. Every great man of God has been a man of prayer first—and then came his usefulness to God.

How God will use you is up to Him. You may not yet see how He's leading you, but if you wait on Him in prayer, the road ahead will become clearer and clearer.

When in prayer, whether short or long, simply stay on your knees until you're satisfied that God has uttered His "Amen" before you offer your own.

"Hurry is the death of prayer." —SAMUEL CHADWICK

Strength out of Weakness

And he said unto me, My grace is sufficient for thee: for my strength is made perfect in weakness. Most gladly therefore will I rather glory in my infirmities, that the power of Christ may rest upon me (2 Corinthians 12:9).

Wise is the Christian man who's willing to own his weaknesses. We all have them—and not just a few. Thank God we also have our strengths too. And many of the latter are actually found when we look to our weaknesses as a means of trusting in the power of Christ within us.

We can glory in our infirmities only when we see them as opportunities to allow Christ's power to make our strength perfect through our weaknesses. Thank God that today, right now, this very moment, the power of Christ rests on us. We're thus enabled to face anything, especially our weaknesses.

"Before He furnishes the abundant supply, we must first be made conscious of our emptiness. Before he gives strength, we must be made to feel our weakness. Slow, painfully slow, are we to learn this lesson; and slower still to own our nothingness and take the place of helplessness before the Mighty One."
—A.W. Pink

THE MAN OF VISION

Where there is no vision, the people perish (PROVERBS 29:18).

A visionless Christian man is like a boat without a rudder, drifting aimlessly along life's long river. How much more rewarding is the Christian life with a God-given purpose.

What vision has God given you for your life? It need not be spelled out in its entirety—in fact, it rarely is. Yet like a headlight on the highway shining just so far, as we move along following the headlight, we can make it safely home.

A vision may begin very small, like a planted seed. Nourished by prayer and with proper follow-through (only as far as the headlight shows the way), the vision for usefulness by God can be attained.

Your vision may be to be a godly husband raising a wholesome family or to own a business that prospers enough to support Christian workers. Truth to tell, there are as many diverse visions for Christian men as there are Christian men.

"We need a baptism of clear seeing. We desperately need seers who can see through the mist—Christian leaders with prophetic vision. Unless they come soon it will be too late for this generation." —A.W. TOZER

THOROUGHLY HIS

Ye are not your own…For ye are bought with a price (1 CO-
RINTHIANS 6:19-20).

The man who soon learns he belongs to God, not to himself, is on the road to happiness. It's in our own ownership that we find trouble. We find our natural desires are at war with the man God has called us to be. When we no longer claim ownership of ourselves, we become free to be better men—God's men in this broken world.

In every facet of our lives, we must surrender our right to self to the one who has purchased us. We must allow Him to do His will with us—and lead us to greater depths of true happiness.

We are His. Wholly His.

Relish in His ownership of you.

"I am His by purchase and I am His by conquest; I am His by donation and I am His by election; I am His by covenant and I am His by marriage; I am wholly His; I am peculiarly His; I am universally His; I am eternally His." —THOMAS BROOKS

CLEANSED FROM ALL SIN

*If we walk in the light, as he is in the light, we have fellow-
ship with one another, and the blood of Jesus Christ his Son
cleanseth us from all sin* (1 JOHN 1:7).

*A*ll sin? Many men would love to believe that all their
sins have been cleansed by the blood of Christ, yet
guilt for past misdeeds lingers on, often simply lurking
in the background of their consciousness.

They may even give mental assent to God's forgiveness of all their sins. And yet, even a molecule of remain-
ing guilt can keep a man from enjoying the truth of full
forgiveness for all sins.

Whether you have this nagging sensation of remain-
ing sins to be forgiven or not, it's always a good thing to
contemplate the vastness of God's love for us in pouring out the blood of Christ so all our sins could be forever removed.

Contemplate today this vastness with profound
thanks for such an atonement.

*"It's Satan's delight to tell me that once he's got me, he will keep
me. But at that moment I can go back to God. And I know
that if I confess my sins, God is faithful and just to forgive me."*
—ALAN REDPATH

SMALL THINGS

Even the very hairs of your head are all numbered. Fear not therefore: ye are of more value than many sparrows (LUKE 12:7).

Every life has its ups and downs, its large things and small things. But does God see anything in our lives as "small"? If He troubles Himself to number the hairs on our head, if He cares when the sparrow falls, will He not watch over our so-called small things with the same attention as if they were large?

Nothing about God's care for us is minor—it's all major. His attention to the details of our lives goes mostly unnoticed by us, but in eternity, we may find that some very small things were the pivotal points at which God worked a large thing without our knowing it.

Trust God for all things, large and small.

"There's no such thing as 'chance,' 'luck,' or 'accident' in the Christian's journey through this world! If we profess to be believers in Jesus Christ—then all is arranged and appointed by God...Let us seek to have an abiding sense of God's hand in all that befalls us. Let us strive to realize that our Father's hand is measuring out our daily portion." —J.C. RYLE

Do the Word

Be ye doers of the word, and not hearers only, deceiving your own selves (JAMES 1:22).

To hear something takes very little effort. We can sit passively and listen to a message, program, or even the Bible on Audible. But *doing* what we've heard—well, that's a different story.

We can hear and *not* do—which the Bible labels as self-deception. And while it's true we're never saved by our works but only by faith, it's a faith that bears fruit.

It's up to each of us to hear from God and then do what we've been told. For some, the doing is about helping others. For others, it's about supporting those who are helping others. No man is left with nothing to do while he's here on earth. All Christian men are fruit-bearing trees.

"The man who hears Christian teaching, and practices what he hears…doesn't content himself with listening to exhortations to repent, believe in Christ, and live a holy life. He actually repents. He actually believes. He actually ceases to do evil, learns to do well, abhors that which is sinful, and cleaves to that which is good. He is a doer as well as a hearer." —J.C. RYLE

A MAN'S ANGER

A wrathful man stirreth up strife: but he that is slow to anger appeaseth strife (PROVERBS 15:18).

Be ye angry, and sin not: let not the sun go down upon your wrath (EPHESIANS 4:26).

Anger in a man is a valid emotion. God experiences anger (though He's slow to anger). Jesus certainly demonstrated anger. Anger has its uses. But when we allow anger to fester, it turns into sin. Anger issues need to be resolved quickly—or as Paul tells us—before the sun goes down.

A Christian man has ways of handling anger that many men do not. For instance, if we are sinned against and hold a grudge or find a grudge against us, we go to that brother or to the church for resolution (Matthew 18). Another option is an appropriate compromise. Repentance and forgiveness are, of course, the ultimate resolutions to anger.

In any case, a Christian man is to control his anger, not be controlled by it—or by any emotion. Today, monitor your emotions—particularly if anger has been a problem in your life.

"Anger is short-lived in a good man." —THOMAS FULLER

A Thankful Spirit

In every thing give thanks: for this is the will of God in Christ Jesus concerning you (1 THESSALONIANS 5:18).

Thankfulness is necessary for true happiness. Many of us express our gratitude to God when things are going well. But having a thankful spirit means we've learned to be thankful at all times and in all circumstances. When the circumstances are adverse, we know we can be thankful because God will bring us through in His time. It's during these times of circumstantial famine that we most need the continual feast of a thankful and contented spirit.

It can take time to learn true thankfulness. But God is patient and continues to send circumstances our way in which we can practice thankfulness—no matter how we feel.

Feast on contentment. Feast on thankfulness to God.

"A thankful and a contented spirit is a continual feast. We ought to be contented, and we shall be contented, if we are in the habit of seeing God in everything, and living upon Him day by day. Oh, for a spirit of true thankfulness!"
—ASHTON OXENDEN

FRIENDS

Iron sharpeneth iron; so a man sharpeneth the countenance of his friend (PROVERBS 27:17).

The soul of Jonathan was knit with the soul of David, and Jonathan loved him as his own soul (1 SAMUEL 18:1).

Solid male friendships seem to be rare these days. The closeness of David and Jonathan seems unattainable. And yet most men would welcome more and deeper friendships with other men. They desire the kind of iron-sharpening-iron friendships that make each man stronger.

Often, time is the enemy of friendship. We have our jobs and our family responsibilities…so *when* is the time for developing friendships?

It's like anything else we deem important. If it's something we truly want, we'll make time for it, even if it means cutting back on something else. It also takes initiative. Someone has to suggest a next move toward friendship. A fishing trip? Bowling? Guys' movie-night out? Prayer and Bible study? The best options are those that allow time to simply talk to one another, getting to know the other guy as he probably wants to be known.

What part can you play in fostering a deepening relationship with some man you suspect would make a good friend?

"A good friend is my nearest relation." —THOMAS FULLER

Only God...

Jesus beheld them, and said unto them, With men this is impossible; but with God all things are possible (MATTHEW 19:26).

Every Christian man experiences hard times and intense trials when nothing but a miracle will do. What seems impossible for us can only be made possible by a God who is all-powerful and at the ready to oversee our victories.

Never be alarmed at "only God" circumstances. They build our faith and, as a by-product, they produce compassion in us for others who suffer through the rough patches of life.

If we know the power of God in our lives, we practice turning "only God" situations over to Him.

"God loves with a great love the man whose heart is bursting with a passion for the impossible." —WILLIAM BOOTH

THE ULTIMATE MAN CAVE

He that dwelleth in the secret place of the most High shall abide under the shadow of the Almighty (PSALM 91:1).

Psalm 91 is the perfect spiritual man cave and a great go-to portion of Scripture for men who have been shaken by life's events and who yearn for unshakeable stability during tough times. It's printed on the next two pages.

Christian men become unshakeable by being protected by an unshakeable God. We know nothing can harm us that doesn't pass through God's notice first. We are confident in knowing God has our backs. He's our fortress, our refuge, our man cave. He covers us with His feathers, His truth is our shield and buckler. We're not afraid of terror by night nor daytime's poisoned arrows aimed at us. No pestilence can touch us, nor can destruction alarm us.

This unshakeable confidence is our legacy, and we will live and die by it.

"Faith is a living and unshakable confidence, a belief in the grace of God so assured that a man would die a thousand deaths for its sake." —MARTIN LUTHER

PSALM 91

He that dwelleth in the secret place of the most High shall abide under the shadow of the Almighty.

I will say of the LORD, He is my refuge and my fortress: my God; in him will I trust.

Surely he shall deliver thee from the snare of the fowler, and from the noisome pestilence.

He shall cover thee with his feathers, and under his wings shalt thou trust: his truth shall be thy shield and buckler.

Thou shalt not be afraid for the terror by night; nor for the arrow that flieth by day;

Nor for the pestilence that walketh in darkness; nor for the destruction that wasteth at noonday.

A thousand shall fall at thy side, and ten thousand at thy right hand; but it shall not come nigh thee.

Only with thine eyes shalt thou behold and see the reward of the wicked.

Because thou hast made the LORD, which is my refuge, even the most High, thy habitation;

There shall no evil befall thee, neither shall any plague come nigh thy dwelling.

For he shall give his angels charge over thee, to keep thee in all thy ways.

They shall bear thee up in their hands, lest thou dash thy foot against a stone.

Thou shalt tread upon the lion and adder: the young lion and the dragon shalt thou trample under feet.

Because he hath set his love upon me, therefore will I deliver him: I will set him on high, because he hath known my name.

He shall call upon me, and I will answer him: I will be with him in trouble; I will deliver him, and honor him.

With long life will I satisfy him, and show him my salvation.

DELIGHTING IN GOD

Delight thyself also in the LORD: and he shall give thee the desires of thine heart (PSALM 37:4).

O taste and see that the LORD is good: blessed is the man that trusteth in him (PSALM 34:8).

God has a wonderful way of giving us the desires of our hearts. He encourages us to delight ourselves in Him and in those things that delight Him. He invites us to taste of Him and be satisfied.

Delighting in God is no sour chore.

Delighting in God is its own reward and is the avenue to the desires of our own hearts.

To delight in God is to simply and earnestly *enjoy* Him.

"To wait on God is to live a life of desire toward Him, delight in Him, dependence on Him, and devotedness to Him."
—MATTHEW HENRY

LIVING TO THE GLORY OF GOD

Whether therefore ye eat, or drink, or whatsoever ye do, do all to the glory of God (1 CORINTHIANS 10:31).

God, in His infinite creativity, has chosen a specific way for each of us to glorify Him through our lives. Perhaps it's by being a creator—a writer, painter, sculptor, inventor. Or maybe our way to glorify God is by living to help others. Or by being a faithful husband and father.

Take a moment and consider how your calling in life can best glorify God.

It's when others see Christ glorified in you that they will be drawn to Him. Sometimes the best witness we can be simply involves living righteously.

"We glorify God by living lives that honor Him." —BILLY GRAHAM

I CAN DO THIS!

I can do all things through Christ which strengtheneth me (PHILIPPIANS 4:13).

We all encounter times when we must do what we don't want to do or feel we can't do. We don't feel up for the challenge. And yet what is our faith worth if it doesn't enable us to triumph during the worst of times?

A man with small faith may skate through an easy life. A man of true faith puts aside his fears and displays bravery in the face of adversity. His knees may be shaking, but he's up for this challenge because he knows his God will strengthen him through all things.

If this is not your day for a challenge, don't rest so easy. Your day, like mine, like that of all men, will soon be upon you. And you will prevail as you do "all things."

"If we desire our faith to be strengthened, we should not shrink from opportunities where our faith may be tried, and therefore, through trial, be strengthened." —GEORGE MÜLLER

PREPARING OUR WAYS

[Jotham] did that which was right in the sight of the LORD, according to all that his father Uzziah did…So Jotham became mighty, because he prepared his ways before the LORD his God (2 CHRONICLES 27:2,6).

Jotham was a young man of twenty-five when he took the throne. Following in his father Uzziah's footsteps, he did that which was right in the sight of the Lord. Further, he became mighty for one reason: *He prepared his ways before the Lord.*

Who among us would be mighty in God's eyes? It's no small reward to be pleasing to God. The reward is eternal and in many cases, such as Jotham's, also temporal. He became a rich man and the winner of many wars. Though he only served sixteen years and then died, he is, to this day, reckoned as a mighty man.

Let each of us take care to prepare our ways—and our days—before the Lord.

"[Jotham] walked circumspectly and with much caution, contrived how to shun that which was evil and compass that which was good. He…established or fixed his ways before the Lord, that is, he walked steadily and constantly in the way of his duty, was uniform and resolute in it." —MATTHEW HENRY

HE IS WORTHY!

The four and twenty elders fall down before him that sat on the throne, and worship him that liveth for ever and ever, and cast their crowns before the throne, saying, Thou art worthy, O Lord, to receive glory and honor and power: for thou hast created all things, and for thy pleasure they are and were created (REVELATION 4:10-11).

John, in his exile to Patmos, wrote the book of Revelation and there offers us the words of praise the four and twenty elders uttered. It's not a bad place for us to start our own praise session. We simply declare His worthiness and verbally ascribe honor and power to Him for His creation. Then we keep going by offering praise for specific blessings, but most of all we praise Him for who He is...for His very worthiness.

A day without praise is a day to regret.

"If you had a thousand crowns you should put them all on the head of Christ! And if you had a thousand tongues they should all sing his praise, for he is worthy!" —WILLIAM TIPTAFT

THE CREATIVE MAN

Moses said unto the children of Israel, See, the LORD hath…
filled [Bezaleel] with the spirit of God, in wisdom, in under-
standing, and in knowledge, and in all manner of workman-
ship; and to devise curious works, to work in gold, and in
silver, and in brass, and in the cutting of stones…and in carv-
ing of wood, to make any manner of cunning work (EXO-
DUS 35:30-33).

It pleasures God to invest talent in His sons. Some talents are in the arts (painting, music, poetry), some
are in the manual arts (woodworking, metalworking,
masonry), and some are design-related or mechanical in
nature. Often, these talents are overlooked as being gifts
from God, but happy is the man who perceives his gift
and uses it in ways that please God.

If your gift isn't apparent to you, ask God. It may
have yet to unfold in your life, or it may be dormant for
lack of use. It need not be flashy—God provides talents
large and small. It's not the size, it's the giving out of one's
gift that counts.

"Time is lost when we have not lived a full human life, time
unenriched by experience, creative endeavor, enjoyment, and
suffering."—DIETRICH BONHOEFFER

GENEROSITY

He that hath pity upon the poor lendeth unto the LORD; and that which he hath given will he pay him again (PROVERBS 19:17).

Astingy or miserly Christian man is an oxymoron. God has so designed His godly men to be cheerful givers—even lavish givers. This is often counter to what the world expects us to be. We're told by our culture to become rich, to accumulate more money…but to what end? A rich man dies and takes nothing with him to the grave. A godly man dies and finds an investment in heaven that has earned significant interest.

What needs do you see that you can help meet? Who in your church needs an anonymous gift? Make it your practice to give more than to get more.

God will show you where to give.

"We sometimes forget that nothing is given to us for ourselves alone. When abundance of blessing or prosperity in any form comes to us, we may not shut ourselves in with it, and use it only for ourselves. We are to think of those outside who have no such blessing or favor as we are enjoying, and are to send portions to them." —J.R. MILLER

SAFE MEN

This is the will of God, even your sanctification, that ye should abstain from fornication: That every one of you should know how to possess his vessel in sanctification and honor (1 THESSALONIANS 4:3-4).

A godly man is a *safe* man. Safe around women, children, and even other men. We guard the personhood of anyone who is threatened, especially those who are threatened sexually through abuse or rape. We are protectors of the vulnerable, never perpetrators. Our common fellowship with other believing men is a fellowship with other safe men.

When innocence is violated, we do not let it pass unnoticed. Sin is not hidden by the safe man. Not only are *we* safe, but we see to it that we're raising safe sons and teaching young men to be safe.

Take pride in being a safe man. For to protect others is to emulate the divine protection God affords us. He is a safe God, and we are His safe men.

"The most critical need of the church at this moment is men, bold men, free men. The church must seek, in prayer and much humility, the coming again of men made of the stuff of which prophets and martyrs are made." —A.W. TOZER

Lights in the World

That ye may be blameless and harmless, the sons of God, without rebuke, in the midst of a crooked and perverse nation, among whom ye shine as lights in the world (Philippians 2:15).

A Christian man doesn't have to search for evil. Rather, evil searches out the godly man. The influences are all too close to us in the form of TV, movies, song lyrics, books…But are we just men focused on uncovering evil?

No, we must be men who both avoid evil and pursue good. We're to be blameless and harmless sons of God in the midst of a perverse generation. We're to overcome evil with good. So let's train our eyes to look for righteousness and goodness in our world.

Evil may be easier to spot, but it's more rewarding to see and affirm the good.

Watch for a way today to affirm goodness around you.

"The great and important duty which is incumbent on Christians, is to guard against all appearance of evil; to watch against the first risings in the heart to evil; and to have a guard upon our actions, that they may not be sinful, or so much as seem to be so." —George Whitefield

VYING FOR THE CROWN

Henceforth there is laid up for me a crown of righteousness, which the Lord, the righteous judge, shall give me at that day: and not to me only, but unto all them also that love his appearing (2 TIMOTHY 4:8).

The secret to getting through a rough patch in life is to look longingly ahead to eternity. We are on this earth but a scant few years compared to what awaits us after we move on to our heavenly home. Paul suffered much for the gospel, including stoning, whippings, scarcities, rejection, and ultimately a martyr's death. But he counted it all worthwhile for the reward that awaited him. Paul goes on to say that the same reward awaits all who love Christ's appearing.

So yes, we look ahead to that day of His appearing, and the crown that shall be ours.

"There are no crown-wearers in heaven who were not cross-bearers here below." —CHARLES SPURGEON

GENERATION TO GENERATION

One generation shall praise thy works to another, and shall declare thy mighty acts (PSALM 145:4).

Every Christian man has a duty to the generations below him. Even if we're not a father of sons, we can be father-like to younger men coming up in the faith. A thirty-something-year-old man can have a strong influence on a ten-year-old. A man in his fifties can help a twenty-year-old become all he's meant to be. A man in his seventies and beyond can influence several generations below him.

Consider how God has orchestrated events in your life for your good. Tell your story to other men, including younger men. Be willing to teach the younger men around you—at church, in the home, in the workplace. Reach out with a hand to help the younger man up the mountain. You may think you're influencing just one man, but through his future influence, you may be reaching more than you think. Take up the task of helping other males into manhood.

"Oh! young men, learn to be thoughtful. Learn to consider what you are doing—and where you are going. Make time for calm reflection. Commune with your own heart—and be still." —J.C. RYLE

A Man's Conscience

Let us draw near with a true heart in full assurance of faith, having our hearts sprinkled from an evil conscience, and our bodies washed with pure water (HEBREWS 10:22).

One crucial prerequisite for confidence in the presence of God is a clear conscience. At no time should we be aware of unrepented sin. Keep short accounts with God. When you've violated your conscience, own up to it. Confess it to God and, by faith, accept His forgiveness—and then move on. Once sin is forsaken and confessed, the deed is done. You never have to ask for forgiveness for the same sin twice. (The second asking only reveals a lack of faith that God forgave you at the first asking.)

Then *do* draw near. Do pray with confidence. As sure as God heard your confession, He now hears your requests. There is a righteous boldness before God that belongs to every Christian man, and God loves spiritual boldness in His sons.

"Preserve your conscience always soft and sensitive. If but one sin force its way into that tender part of the soul and dwell there, the road is paved for a thousand iniquities." —ISAAC WATTS

THE LOVE OF MONEY

The love of money is the root of all evil: which while some coveted after, they have erred from the faith, and pierced themselves through with many sorrows (1 TIMOTHY 6:10).

Coveting money is a shortcut to spiritual suicide. If we desire riches, we'll surely find ways to have them. But we'll eventually discover that on the other side of our pot of gold is a bucket of sorrows money can't buy our way out of.

A wise man will avoid the inevitable piercing of many sorrows by seeking God first and foremost, trusting that all needed material goods, including finances, will be supplied through the work God gives us to do or from the hands of those who care for us.

The word "love" is best used in reference to God and to other people, never to money.

"Do not think me mad. It is not to make money that I believe a Christian should live. The noblest thing a man can do is, just humbly to receive, and then go amongst others and give."
—DAVID LIVINGSTONE

GOSSIP

A talebearer revealeth secrets: but he that is of a faithful spirit concealeth the matter (PROVERBS 11:13).

A froward man soweth strife: and a whisperer separateth chief friends (PROVERBS 16:28).

Women often suffer from the accusation of being gossipers. The truth is, men, too, can be guilty of gossip. Many men say things that should remain unsaid. Rumors, unsubstantiated accusations, and innuendoes are all ways some men fall prey to the sin of gossiping. Friendships suffer, innocents are besmirched, reputations suffer…and all from needless talk.

Most men value the ear of a trusted friend who will never betray a word spoken in confidence. Every man must ask himself if he's that kind of friend. And when gossip or rumor comes to your ears, let it stop there. It need go no farther.

"A gossip is one who tells stories which ought not to be told, whether true or false, whether fairly or unfairly represented. The worst kind of gossips are those who tell their stories to those who are most likely to be provoked by them, and at the same time do not wish to be mentioned as authors of the story, or witnesses in it." —GEORGE LAWSON

Mutual Confession

Confess your faults one to another, and pray one for another, that ye may be healed (JAMES 5:16).

Who in your life can you freely confess your faults to? Who will pray for you when you need God's intervention? Are you the man other men can rely on for brotherly confession and healing prayer?

Many men mistakenly believe it's a weakness to confess their faults to another man, but the opposite is true. A weak man harbors his secrets to himself, unwilling to open up to another man. A strong man finds it easier to admit his failings and seek prayer. He knows that God works through his brothers in Christ.

It doesn't take much to be a faithful man to other faithful men. Be that man. Someone needs your prayers. And you need someone to know your faults prayerfully.

"Sometimes it may be of good use to Christians to disclose their...weaknesses and infirmities to one another, where there are great intimacies and friendships, and where they may help each other by their prayers to obtain pardon of their sins and power against them. Those who make confession of their faults one to another should thereupon pray with and for one another." —MATTHEW HENRY

Judging Others

Therefore thou art inexcusable, O man, whosoever thou art that judgest: for wherein thou judgest another, thou condemnest thyself; for thou that judgest doest the same things. But we are sure that the judgment of God is according to truth against them which commit such things. And thinkest thou this, O man, that judgest them which do such things, and doest the same, that thou shalt escape the judgment of God? (Romans 2:1-3).

It's freeing to realize that the responsibility for judging others isn't up to us. We will therefore neither judge others nor expect others to judge us. Our judge and theirs is God alone. Paul points out to the believers in Rome that they're especially guilty of misjudging others because they're doing the very same things they're judging others for!

May God give us a clear eye to not only forgive others who may offend but also not judge them. The burden of judging is a heavy one. Too heavy for any of us.

"In judging of others, a man laboreth in vain, often erreth and easily sinneth; but in judging and examining himself, he always laboreth fruitfully." —Thomas à Kempis

AMBITION

Whosoever shall exalt himself shall be abased; and he that shall humble himself shall be exalted (MATTHEW 23:12).

Ambition, rightly understood, is a good thing. There are aspects of a man's life in which he should be ambitious. The use of spiritual gifts, for instance. He may be ambitious in sports, desiring to best his record. He may be ambitious at his job as he does his work as unto the Lord. He may be ambitious in ministry, helping others in their Christian walk. Certainly in his family life, a godly man is ambitious to be the best dad and husband he can be.

There is, of course, the wrong use of ambition. The source of wrong ambition is *self.* A man who aspires to greater things to satisfy his ego is approaching ambition in the wrong spirit.

Godly ambition will be motivated by thinking of others or by seeing God glorified through achievement. This involves humbling oneself and allowing God to promote us in our field of ambition as we work hard and wait hard for God to do the promoting.

"Sin comes when we take a perfectly natural desire or longing or ambition and try desperately to fulfill it without God."
—AUGUSTINE

SPEAK TRUTH

Ye shall know the truth, and the truth shall make you free (JOHN 8:32).

Wherefore putting away lying, speak every man truth with his neighbor: for we are members one of another (EPHESIANS 4:25).

We, of all men, must be men of the truth. We are done with falsehoods and compromises with the truth. Yes, being a man of truth will sometimes be hard. Many of our acquaintances don't want to hear the truth if it contradicts what they already believe. In order for the truth we speak to have gravitas, we ourselves must be men with gravitas. Our lives must be examples of the truths we speak and live.

Today you may find a chance to speak a truth that's not popular. If speaking up is appropriate, do so with grace and integrity. The worst response to hearing a lie is to passively give the impression you agree with the untruth being spoken or acted upon.

Remember that the truth will set us free. It's the lies we encounter that lay us low.

"He that takes truth for his guide, and duty for his end, may safely trust to God's providence to lead him aright." —BLAISE PASCAL

CORRUPT SPEECH

Let no corrupt communication proceed out of your mouth, but that which is good to the use of edifying, that it may minister grace unto the hearers (EPHESIANS 4:29).

But now ye also put off all these; anger, wrath, malice, blasphemy, filthy communication out of your mouth (COLOSSIANS 3:8).

When we were saved, our mouths were saved along with the rest of us. Every part of our being is to be submitted to God. When it comes to our tongues, submission to God means we weigh our words before we speak. We do not speak corruption, lies, anger, blasphemy, or filthiness. Instead, we speak good words that edify and bring grace to those with whom we speak.

If, due to long-held habit, our words have not been edifying, we can establish a new habit—by *learning* to speak affirming words (and corrective words too) when appropriate. One way to ingrain the habit of speaking that which is good is to consciously look for opportunities to compliment or affirm someone else. Seek such an opportunity today.

"In our manner of speech, our plans of living, our dealings with others, our conduct and walk in the church and out of it; all should be done as becomes the gospel." —ALBERT BARNES

Racism

For there is no difference between the Jew and the Greek: for the same Lord over all is rich unto all that call upon him (ROMANS 10:12).

God's method of dividing mankind has nothing to do with race. God saves all who trust in Christ, with no racial distinction. Christians, by virtue of their new nature, should know this instinctively.

A Christian cannot be a racist. It violates the very idea of a God who is "Lord over all, and is rich to all what call upon him." Neither can a Christian affirm those who espouse or support racism. With God, every racial barrier is down. Jews, Gentiles of all colors, are accepted based on their faith in Christ. To erect any other kind of barrier where God has torn down a barrier is to foolishly try to trump God Himself.

Christian men rejoice in the God who sees the heart, not the color of a man's skin. Such men also rejoice in their brothers of another color.

"Be not proud of race, face, place, or grace." —CHARLES SPURGEON

SECRET SIN

Thou hast set our iniquities before thee, our secret sins in the light of thy countenance (PSALM 90:8).

What a man does publicly is important, but what a man does in secret reveals his true character. When we're tempted to commit a sin no one will ever know about, what's our response? For some, the decision is easy. We can sin, no one will know, and God will forgive.

That sort of thinking is selfish, self-wounding, and presumptuous. When we sin in the dark, we hurt our souls by partaking of actions or attitudes that war against our better selves.

Will God forgive secret sin? Yes, but inherent in God's forgiveness is repentance on our part. True sorrow works a repentant attitude in us. Such an attitude rebels at the next thought of secret sin and rejects it. This is the building of true character in a man. Too, we must be aware that secret sin will eventually lead to open sin.

"There are no sins so pernicious to the souls of men as those that are most inward and secret. Secret sins often reign in the souls of men most powerfully, when they are least apparent!"
—THOMAS BROOKS

Spiritual Gifts

Every man hath his proper gift of God, one after this manner, and another after that (1 Corinthians 7:7).

As every man hath received the gift, even so minister the same one to another, as good stewards of the manifold grace of God (1 Peter 4:10).

It seems remarkable that so many men wonder what their "proper gift" from God is. Many may even wonder if indeed they have such a gift. But we're reminded by Scripture that "every man hath received the gift," with the responsibility to minister that gift for the benefit of others.

How then does one discover and develop their spiritual gift? First, by simply asking God. Then by considering where we find joy in serving. What do others see as our giftedness? Though the "proper gift" may be given at the moment of conversion, it may be revealed to us over the course of time. But we must be desiring our gifts and willing to use them. God will not give us gifts we will not use.

"Do not bury the gifts and talents which have been given to you, but use them, that you may enter into the joy of your Lord."
—Sadhu Sundar Singh

GROUNDED MEN

Be not conformed to this world: but be ye transformed by the renewing of your mind (ROMANS 12:2).

Before we knew Christ, we were fashioned after the course of the Christ-rejecting world. We took our cues on manhood from sitcoms, glossy magazines, social media, and ad campaigns promoting a sense of manhood far different from God's design. And it's in God's design for us as men that we find happiness, purpose, and a fruitful destiny.

We never fully grasp all God has for us as men, but as we pursue Him and His purposes, He reveals more and more of His plan. We have only to respond to God—the Great Initiator of our destiny. We need only to be assured of our place as God's men in the unfolding of history.

"Uncertainty as to our relationship with God is one of the most enfeebling and dispiriting of things. It makes a man heartless. It takes the pith out of him. He cannot fight; he cannot run. He is easily dismayed and gives way. He can do nothing for God. But when we know that we are of God, we are vigorous, brave, invincible. There is no more quickening truth than this of assurance." —HORATIUS BONAR

In Understanding Be Men

Brethren, be not children in understanding: howbeit in malice be ye children, but in understanding be men (1 CORINTHIANS 14:20).

Every man faces circumstances that are, at the time, not understandable. We may have doubts about God's way of doing things. We may question His goodness. We may wonder at His motives. But as we mature as men, as we become more acquainted with His ways, we grow into men of understanding. Not necessarily the circumstances God has arranged, but the character of God Himself. He who can do no wrong always works out His will to our ultimate benefit.

"Faith is the deliberate confidence in the character of God whose ways you may not understand at the time."—OSWALD CHAMBERS

OUR INHERITANCE

And if children, then heirs; heirs of God, and joint-heirs with Christ; if so be that we suffer with him, that we may be also glorified together (ROMANS 8:17).

Because we are God's children, we are also his heirs. We have obtained a divine inheritance and that inheritance is priceless. All we have in this life and the next is found in Christ. As we learn to dwell by faith in Him, we learn more and more about our inheritance. We discover we don't need money to be rich—the High King of heaven is our treasure. When we make Him so, we prosper. Not necessarily monetarily, but according to God's definition of prosperity. But if we are to inherit and share His glory, we will also share His suffering. Learning to suffer is not pleasant, but when we suffer for any reason—whether it's our own foolish mistakes, addictions, or unforeseen circumstances—we have "glory" waiting for us on the other side of our suffering.

"Riches I heed not, nor man's empty praise, / thou mine inheritance, now and always: / thou and thou only, first in my heart, / High King of heaven, my treasure thou art." —"BE THOU MY VISION," ATTRIBUTED TO DALLAN FORGAILL

GOD IN CREATION

The heavens declare the glory of God; and the firmament showeth his handywork. Day unto day uttereth speech, and night unto night showeth knowledge (PSALM 19:1-2).

God's glory in creation is dazzling. It brings health and healing to our deepest wounds. Nature isn't always readily accessible, but surely some part of God's creative world can be visited. Allow the beauty of the world outside of man's creations to renew your mind. Stop somewhere and drink in the beautiful surroundings. Then consider the God who created it—and you, as His greater creation. Worship Him silently as you ponder His world and your unique place in it. Give thanks.

"The spiritual mind, fond of soaring through nature in quest of new proofs of God's existence and fresh emblems of His wisdom, power and goodness—exults in the thought that it is his Father's domain which he treads! He feels that God, his God, is there." —OCTAVIUS WINSLOW

PERFECT AND COMPLETE

Knowing this, that the trying of your faith worketh patience. But let patience have her perfect work, that ye may be perfect and entire, wanting nothing (JAMES 1:3-4).

The perfect and complete Christian is so because he or she has found their true full, perfect, and complete self in Christ. Men and women without Christ are imperfect and incomplete—no matter how successful they appear on the outside—a fact borne out by the many ways they try to complete their personhood. To be complete is to lack nothing and thus seek happiness in nothing other than Christ. This is the road to the full effect of the measure of perfection we're allowed on earth.

"Through the death of Christ on the cross, making atonement for sin, we get a perfect standing before God. That is justification, and it puts us, in God's sight, back in Eden before sin entered. God looks upon us and treats us as if we had never sinned." —A. C. DIXON

Owned by God

Whether we live, we live unto the Lord; and whether we die, we die unto the Lord: whether we live therefore, or die, we are the Lord's (Romans 14:8).

There is great joy in being owned by God. Most Christian men have already come to the conclusion that ownership of oneself is a nonstarter. Perhaps we suffer a failure or two relationally, vocationally, or financially, or maybe we go through a season of seriously poor health. For some, addiction reveals our inability to be our own keepers. Praise God when our eyes are finally opened to the joy that comes from knowing God owns us and we are here to glorify Him in our bodies, souls, and spirits.

There is no part of us God is unwilling to claim as His own. Every day we have the opportunity to remind both ourselves and God that we belong to Him. How then shall we not rejoice in His care?

"God owns all; He owns me; He owns my home; He owns my children; He owns my property...The Christian idea is this: that God is the absolute owner of all things." —Clovis G. Chappell

THE GOLIATH OF LUST

So David prevailed over the Philistine with a sling and with a stone, and smote the Philistine, and slew him; but there was no sword in the hand of David (1 SAMUEL 17:50).

Facing the Goliath of lust within us can mean only one thing: We will prevail without swords or earthly weapons. We need only to be confidently wielding the sling of faith, filled with the stone of prayer, and our Goliath of lust will fall like a redwood in the forest.

David's mighty brothers weren't up to the job of facing Goliath. It took David, the smallest of the siblings, to defeat the giant. God chooses His warriors among the small, those who will simply have faith. Even against the Goliath of lust.

"Do as David when he was to go up against Goliath. He said, 'I come to you in the name of the Lord!' So say to your Goliath lust, 'I come to you in the name of Christ!' Then we conquer, when the Lion of the tribe of Judah marches before us!"
—THOMAS WATSON

TEMPTATIONS

Watch and pray, that ye enter not into temptation: the spirit indeed is willing, but the flesh is weak (MATTHEW 26:41).

Temptations will always come, and we must be ready for them. Prayer preparation is key to overcoming, for every temptation finds its resistance in prayer. However, we must pray far ahead of the temptation to be fully prepared. To be "prayed up" is to be temptation resistant.

One of the unexpected pluses of temptation is that it creates great prayer warriors. Take your place among God's army of intercessors. Let temptation have the positive effect of exercising your faith. Overcome temptation through prayer to a mighty God.

"Temptation exercises our faith and teaches us to pray."
—A.B. SIMPSON

OBEY WHAT YOU
KNOW YOU NEED TO DO

Samuel said, Hath the LORD as great delight in burnt offer-ings and sacrifices, as in obeying the voice of the LORD? Behold, to obey is better than sacrifice (1 SAMUEL 15:22).

Sacrifice can be a positive part of our Christian life—if it's done in faith and not out of legalism. But bet-ter than sacrifice is obedience. Obedience to what? First of all to what we know is right, defined by the words of Scripture. Second, we must obey the promptings God has given us for our own lives. Many men sense God's calling in one direction only to head off in another direc-tion. Ask Jonah how that turns out.

Obeying, like sacrifice, is done by faith. Obeying God keeps us firmly in God's will and on the right track. Contrarily, disobedience to God's known will can only bring setbacks in our walk with God. Stay the course of obedience and be blessed.

"The Bible recognizes no faith that does not lead to obedience, nor does it recognize any obedience that does not spring from faith. The two are at opposite sides of the same coin." —A.W. TOZER

ENJOY THE BANQUET!

He brought me to the banqueting house, and his banner over me was love (SONG OF SOLOMON 2:4).

The gospel is like a lavish banquet to which all are invited. Sadly, not all come to the table the Lord has spread for them. Even some Christians will sometimes feast on spiritual junk food rather than eat from the healthy and tasty banqueting table. It's true the table isn't easily seen, as is the junk food. God has so arranged the table that one must be hungry for the delicacies He has spread for us.

You may see others content with the lesser food, but your steps should take you beyond the trough. Keep walking and you'll soon be there—worth the effort.

"Jesus has a table spread / Where the saints of God are fed, / He invites His chosen people, 'Come and dine'; / With His manna He doth feed / And supplies our every need: / Oh, 'tis sweet to sup with Jesus all the time! / 'Come and dine,' the Master calleth, 'Come and dine'; / You may feast at Jesus' table all the time; / He Who fed the multitude, turned the water into wine, / To the hungry calleth now, 'Come and dine.'" —CHARLES B. WIDMEYER

SILENT STRENGTH

Be silent, O all flesh, before the LORD: for he is raised up out of his holy habitation (ZECHARIAH 2:13).

There is wisdom in the old adage "Better to be silent and thought a fool rather than to speak and remove all doubt." In a world full of words, a godly man finds strength in silence—both when alone or with others. In silence, we can hear better than when we fill the air with our words. Make silence a strength, not a weakness. When you do speak, let it be seasoned with grace.

"A man who lives right, and is right, has more power in his silence than another has by his words."—PHILLIPS BROOKS

Right Thinking

For God hath not given us the spirit of fear; but of power, and of love, and of a sound mind (2 TIMOTHY 1:7).

Our thoughts can take us where we want to go…or where we don't want to go. In the latter case, a random but undesired thought may occur to us—often out of nowhere—and if we allow that thought to take root, we can end up turning those thoughts into actions we later regret.

Wise is the man who controls his thoughts, rejecting negative or destructive thoughts the second they occur. Wise, too, is the man who welcomes life-affirming thoughts that likewise can turn into actions that advance his spiritual, vocational, or family life. Learn, then, to discipline your mind—the result will be a well-lived life.

"The secret of living a life of excellence is merely a matter of thinking thoughts of excellence. Really, it's a matter of programming our minds with the kind of information that will set us free." —CHUCK SWINDOLL

HAPPY IS THE MAN

Happy is he that hath the God of Jacob for his help, whose hope is in the LORD his God (PSALM 146:5).

Does God desire us to be happy? Let's turn the question around and maybe the answer will be evident. Does God desire us to be *unhappy*? I think most would agree that God's will is not a life of unhappiness. But what of adversity that brings unhappiness into our lives? For the Christian man, adversity must be endured with an end in sight.

Unhappiness is counterproductive, while happiness enhances productivity. True happiness, we know, comes from God, and the happy man is the man who trusts in God, even during adversity. He knows that God can even bring a positive result at the end of any trial. Trust in the final outcome, not in the dubious unfolding of adversity.

"No man in the world should be so happy as a man of God. It is one continual source of gladness. He can look up and say, 'God is my Father, Christ is my Savior, and the Church is my mother.'" —D.L. MOODY

Your Worst Enemy

Look not every man on his own things, but every man also on the things of others (PHILIPPIANS 2:4).

Most men who have had a good look in the mirror will admit that's where they met their greatest enemy. History has seen many a good man falter under the weight of obsessive self-interest. God's prescription for overcoming this mortal enemy is to adopt the habit of turning our eyes toward the needs of others. There are people in every man's life that can benefit from his influence, his presence, or his support. Be that man. Become your own best friend by befriending others.

"I have had more trouble with myself than with any other man I have ever met." —D.L. MOODY

SEALED!

Now he which stablisheth us with you in Christ, and hath anointed us, is God; Who hath also sealed us, and given the earnest of the Spirit in our hearts (2 CORINTHIANS 1:21-22).

Every man in Christ has a seal about him. This seal was given by the Holy Spirit and is one of the markers of belonging to God. From what are we sealed? We're sealed *from* the world and its anti-Christian influence and sealed *to* God and His kingdom.

When temptations arise, it's imperative to remember that though we're not sealed from temptations, we are sealed from having to act on them. We are given ways of escape. We have the ability to remind Satan that our seal is like a boundary he cannot cross. Our seal, then, becomes yet one more advantage we have in living a positive Christian life.

"Come, blessed and eternal Spirit, into my heart; make it a temple, now and forever, for Your abode worthless though the offering be, yet it is all I have to present You; enter, with all Your humbling, sanctifying, sealing and comforting influences, and take full possession for Yourself." —OCTAVIUS WINSLOW

GOD CONFIDENCE

And now, little children, abide in him; that, when he shall appear, we may have confidence, and not be ashamed before him at his coming (1 JOHN 2:28).

A foolish man who doesn't know his God will trust in himself to get through life successfully. The Christian man knows better. He knows his weaknesses and has confidence in God. This confidence enables him to make the right decisions, keep his temper, act appropriately in every situation, and flourish under pressure. Confidence in God is often learned over the course of time. It's been appreciated when circumstances remind us of our own fallibility.

Confidence in God comes, too, through simple faith. Faith that God knows all, sees all, and that His hand is working behind the scenes in every aspect of our lives.

"The ultimate ground of faith and knowledge is confidence in God." —CHARLES HODGE

LIVE BY THE POWER

But ye shall receive power, after that the Holy Ghost is come upon you: and ye shall be witnesses unto me both in Jerusalem, and in all Judaea, and in Samaria, and unto the uttermost part of the earth (ACTS 1:8).

Many Christian men live by the power of their own human strength. Human strength is good, but it's not enough. The believing man has access to power beyond his natural strength. That power is found in the indwelling Holy Spirit. When we rely on Him, we're able to access resources beyond what the natural man can obtain. Sadly, many men neglect to use it.

Christian men, in a darkening age, must learn to live God-filled and God-led lives. Nothing less will do. How then do we access this supernatural strength? By appropriating each day's strength (and wisdom and discernment) through faith anew every morning. Reading and trusting in the power of God's Word is imperative. As we take in God's Word, we are refueled and enabled to meet every challenge.

"If you look up into His face and say, 'Yes, Lord, whatever it costs,' at that moment He'll flood your Life with His presence and power." —ALAN REDPATH

May God Be Glorified

That God in all things may be glorified through Jesus Christ, to whom be praise and dominion for ever and ever. Amen (1 Peter 4:11).

The wise Christian man is all about glorifying God. He does this through the way he lives, the work of his hands, the family he leads. This part of a Christian man's job description requires great humility. Men who lead out of pride can cause great harm to themselves and those whom they purpose to lead. Glorifying God requires taking oneself down several notches. We esteem others more than ourselves. We search for ways to serve those in our circle of influence.

Today you may find a God-ordained way to glorify God. Watch for it...and act on it.

"We should always look upon ourselves as God's servants, placed in God's world, to do his work; and accordingly labor faithfully for him; not with a design to grow rich and great, but to glorify God, and do all the good we possibly can."
—David Brainerd

The Great Restorer

He restoreth my soul: he leadeth me in the paths of righteousness for his name's sake (Psalm 23:3).

Our God is the Great Restorer. What we have lost—often due to our own foolishness or by responding to fleshly desires—God desires to heal. The path of healing includes the removal of our painful memories and our guilt over sins long ago forgiven by God as well as the granting of assurance that we have peace with God. Many a man has been held back in life because he has not yet allowed God to restore that which has been lost. Though it doesn't happen in an instant, it happens as God applies His truth as a salve to our wounds.

Don't let another day go by without identifying an area where you need restoration—and then allow God to do His restorative work.

"We often need to have our soul restored, quickened, revived or we would never get safely home, through this evil world."
—J.R. Miller

SEED THOUGHTS

For out of the heart proceed evil thoughts, murders, adulteries, fornications, thefts, false witness, blasphemies (MATTHEW 15:19).

Our departure from God's will for right living usually starts with just a thought, doesn't it? A seed thought that when watered by our carnal desires blossoms into further wrong thoughts, words, and actions. We don't often realize that the summoning up of evil thoughts is the summoning up of Satan's kingdom, his minions, his lies, his strategies. Soon after, subtly perhaps, will follow his depressions, his mental breakdowns, and other maladies from his bag of destruction.

For victory to reign, every man must be quick to stop evil seed thoughts the moment they appear. To hesitate, to entertain the thought is to give it permission to grow. Hasten to put up a barrier—the shield of faith—to repel the fiery darts of the enemy.

"The heart is the great workshop where all sin is produced before it is exposed to open view. The heart is the mint where evil thoughts are coined, before they are current in our words and actions." —GEORGE SWINNOCK

Blessed Is He

Blessed is he whose transgression is forgiven, whose sin is covered (Psalm 32:1).

Dwelling on our past sins, failures, or mistakes is a nonstarter. It accomplishes nothing except to drag us down. Better instead is to allow all those past missteps to serve a positive purpose. One such purpose is to remind us of God's grace toward us. No matter what we name as a past departure from who we want to be, it is all forgiven at the cross. Grace in the life of a Christian man must mean that all our past failures and successes now serve a purpose.

"True happiness consists not in beauty, honor, riches (the world's trinity); but in the forgiveness of sin." —Thomas Watson

GOD IS OURS TO ENJOY

He brought me forth also into a large place; he delivered me, because he delighted in me (PSALM 18:19).

Most men probably don't think of "enjoying" God. And yet the noted Westminster Shorter Catechism reminds believers that the chief end of man is to glorify God and to enjoy Him forever. That chief end is not just for one denomination or followers of one particular doctrine—it's a true statement fit for all believers. The first part—glorifying God—is a way to consider all our daily activities as a means of glorifying Him. The latter end makes real our relationship with God. He is to be worshipped, but He is also to be enjoyed. Wondrous is the thought that God not only desires us to enjoy Him but also delights in enjoying us.

"Man's chief end is to glorify God, and to enjoy Him forever."
—THE WESTMINSTER SHORTER CATECHISM

TRUTH IS OUR GUARDIAN

The LORD is nigh unto all them that call upon him, to all that call upon him in truth (PSALM 145:18).

If we don't believe the truth, we're open to believing a lie. Thus the truth is a defense against accepting the premise and false promise of a lie.

Truth is our great guardian against lies. Filling our minds with the truth of God's Word enables us to identify the lies of the world and refute them. When our guard is down and we listen to lies, we become open to their deceit. The longer we listen, the more likely our abandonment of the truth and our acceptance of the lie.

Christian men must be men who hunger for truth and guard it, lest the bountiful lies become as "truth."

"One never errs more safely than when one errs by too much loving the truth." —AUGUSTINE

GOD IS NEVER SURPRISED

O fear the LORD, ye his saints: for there is no want to them that fear him. The young lions do lack, and suffer hunger: but they that seek the LORD shall not want any good thing (PSALM 34:9-10).

Is there enough truth in the Bible to meet any and every need? Yes, but we must believe this, preach this, live this. Every circumstance in our lives is known by God. He is never surprised. He never thinks, *Wow, I didn't see that coming.* Or *Whoops, how did that happen?*

When we are in an uncomfortable place—when we're going through a rough patch—it's enough for us to bend our knees to God and ask Him to resolve it according to His perfect will. Then we wait and watch—without worry.

"Pray, and let God worry." —MARTIN LUTHER

OUR GREAT SIN-BEARER

Cast thy burden upon the LORD, and he shall sustain thee: he shall never suffer the righteous to be moved (PSALM 55:22).

Only a truly merciful and loving God would invite His children to cast their burdens on Him. If we have sinned, we need not run away from God but instead run toward Him. Though God hates our sin, He has compassion for us and knows the weight our sin bears down on us. Therefore, He bids us cast all our sin upon the Lamb of Sacrifice, our Great Sin-Bearer. Only a true son of God—Jesus—could bear the weight of the world's sin...including *our* sin. Yes, it's all on Him now. Not on us. Rejoice and praise your Great Sin-Bearer.

"Oh, forbid that we should live looking at sin as though it was not removed, instead of looking to you as our great sin-bearer, and sin-remover! Oh, to live assured that our sins are gone, and gone forever; that the eye of justice will rest upon them no more, that the record in the Divine debt-book is perfectly erased, and that when sought for—they shall not be found!"
—JAMES SMITH

THERE'S POWER IN PRAISE

Blessed be the LORD God, the God of Israel, who only doeth wondrous things (PSALM 72:18).

God delights in our worship of Him. But as a bonus, when we worship God, there is inherent in our worship a blessing for us too. When we focus on God in worship, we're taking our minds off our problems. We can't be fully worshipping if we are still clutching our problems and worries to our chests. Praise allows us to release all our burdens.

In addition, praising God somehow brings us fresh spiritual energy—and often physical energy too—to meet life's demands.

Spend time in worship today. Release all your troubles to Him. Give Him thanks for your many victories too. But most of all, praise Him simply for who He is.

God has so arranged it that when we give thanks and gratitude and praise to God, we receive a blessing.

"Trying to work for God without worshipping God results in joyless legalism. Work minus worship magnifies your will power not God's worth. If you try to do things for God without delighting in God you bring dishonor upon God. Serving God without savoring God is lifeless and unreal."
—JOHN PIPER

PURPOSE: THE
SECRET TO HAPPINESS

In whom also we have obtained an inheritance, being pre-destinated according to the purpose of him who worketh all things after the counsel of his own will (EPHESIANS 1:11).

The secret of happiness is to covet no higher plan in the universe than that which is allotted to us—and at the same time, to be content with no *lesser* place than that to which God has purposed for each of us.

To have a happy life, make each day an ongoing discovery and appropriation of God's unique purpose for you. Trusting that God has such a purpose is critical—but it must then result in seeking that purpose also. For to not seek is to not find.

"God has a purpose in every life, and when the soul is completely yielded and acquiescent, He will certainly realize it. Blessed is he who has never thwarted the working of the divine ideal." —F.B. MEYER

THE FEAR OF THE LORD

The fear of the LORD is clean,
enduring for ever (PSALM 19:9).

The fear of God is a wonderful thing. It's a fountain of life, the beginning of knowledge, the hatred of evil, the source of wisdom, and the basis for confidence. Why then would a man not make it a priority to grasp the fear of the Lord…to make that great fear the cornerstone of life?

The fear of God is also "clean, enduring for ever." To know the fear of the Lord is to know the only thing that endures forever. Fear God, but never be afraid of Him.

"Some may think the fear of God breeds sadness; no, it is the inlet to joy! The fear of God is the morning star, which ushers in the sunlight of comfort: 'Walking in the fear of the Lord, and in the comfort of the Holy Spirit' (Acts 9:31). The fear of God has solid joy in it, though not frivolity. God mixes joy with holy fear, that fear may not seem slavish." —THOMAS WATSON

GRACE'S LESSON

The grace of God that bringeth salvation hath appeared to all men, Teaching us that, denying ungodliness and worldly lusts, we should live soberly, righteously, and godly, in this present world (TITUS 2:11-12).

Among the many benefits of the grace of God is its ability to teach us to deny the ungodliness and worldly lusts that surround us daily. We know for certain that legalism fails to teach us to deny ourselves. We see God's law, and though we may wish to obey, our own lusts lead us into the deep weeds of sin.

Grace first restores us and then teaches us, but we must first each be teachable and willing to learn grace's lesson.

"Grace in the heart prevents us from abusing grace in the head—it delivers us from making grace the lackey of sin. Where the grace of God brings salvation to the soul, it works effectually. And what is it that grace teaches? Practical holiness. Grace does not eradicate ungodliness and worldly lusts— but it causes us to deny them." —ARTHUR PINK

Your Calling

We are his workmanship, created in Christ Jesus unto good works, which God hath before ordained that we should walk in them (Ephesians 2:10).

Every man has some aspect of God's will for him for which that man must assume responsibility. We must be attracted to God's plan for us, knowing without a doubt that God's will trumps any ideas we may have for ourselves. Success, then, is fully leaning into and living out God's call, whether it be visible or quiet. There are no large or small callings of God. Your calling is as large as your hopes and dreams.

"Good works are not to be an amusement, but a vocation. We are not to indulge in them occasionally: they are to be the tenor and bent of our lives." —Charles Spurgeon

Strength and Beauty

Honor and majesty are before him: strength and beauty are in his sanctuary (Psalm 96:6).

God is beautiful—did you realize that? We often gaze at a glorious sunset or flowers and marvel at their loveliness. But if we look beyond the evidence of God's beauty in creation, we will see the beauty of God Himself.

Today, ponder gazing upon God. No, we can't do that literally—yet. But we can gaze upon Him spiritually. We can, as the old hymn says, "look into His wonderful face."

Wherever God is, beauty is.

"My Father, supremely good, beauty of all things beautiful."
—Augustine

THE COMPASSION OF THE LORD

When he saw the multitudes, he was moved with compassion on them, because they fainted, and were scattered abroad, as sheep having no shepherd (MATTHEW 9:36).

When we think of Jesus, what words come to mind? We may recall His healing of the sick, His dying on the cross, His forgiveness of sins, His commitment to His disciples. We may think of His anger at the legalistic Pharisees. But when we consider His whole ministry on earth, we find that all His actions were rooted in *compassion*.

When we act on Christ's behalf in loving others, compassion must be at the core of our motives. When Jesus *saw* the crowds, He had compassion. Seeing requires looking.

Today we may come in contact with harassed and helpless people. Let's look for ways to exhibit compassion toward them. When we extend a hand to help others, we are temporarily acting as undershepherds to the Great Shepherd.

"How far you go in life depends on your being tender with the young, compassionate with the aged, sympathetic with the striving and tolerant of the weak and strong. Because someday in your life you will have been all of these." —GEORGE WASHINGTON CARVER

Finding Our Lives by Losing Our Lives

He that findeth his life shall lose it: and he that loseth his life for my sake shall find it (MATTHEW 10:39).

Jesus strikes at the heart of every man's need when He urges us to lose our lives in order to find them. There is no finding life while keeping our own. To give up oneself is no loss; it's a gain.

Self without Christ renders us as incomplete men. If we're still finding value in an unsurrendered life, we have yet to learn a basic lesson about ourselves. The irony is that in surrender, we find the power to live and accomplish much more than if left to ourselves. Today, feel the power inherent in losing your life...and finding true life in Christ.

"Entire renunciation of the world and self prepares us for the entire and perfect salvation of God. Leave all and you shall possess all." —JAMES SMITH

THE THORN

There was given to me a thorn in the flesh, the messenger of Satan to buffet me, lest I should be exalted above measure. For this thing I besought the Lord thrice, that it might depart from me (2 CORINTHIANS 12:7-8).

When confronted by a thorn, we, like Paul, become eager for the thorn to disappear so we can get on with a thornless life. But God's response to us—as it was to Paul—is that the thorn must stay, perhaps for the rest of our lives.

While the thought sounds discouraging, we must remember that Paul was given strength to bear up under his thorn. God will likewise give us the power to do what we're meant to do.

Ask for God to remove your thorn. And if He does, rejoice. And if He doesn't, rejoice. You will still have all the power necessary to run your race well.

"God will deal out the requisite grace in all time of our need. Seated by us like a kind physician, with His hand on our pulse He will watch our weakness, and accommodate the divine supply to our several needs and circumstances. He will not allow the thorn to pierce too far!" —JOHN MACDUFF

AVOID A TOXIC ENVIRONMENT

But every man is tempted, when he is drawn away of his own lust, and enticed (JAMES 1:14).

There are places every Christian man should avoid. There are people Christian men must avoid. These are the places and people that create a hostile and toxic environment for us. Our past history will reveal where and with whom toxicity is bred.

Superman had to avoid kryptonite. We, too, must know the dangers of spiritual kryptonite. If we think there is no danger to us—that we're somehow exempt from toxic exposure—we're dead wrong. Every man alive has his weaknesses. Wise men know this and build safeguards to keep themselves strong. The best safeguard of all is avoidance of danger. It would be good to make a list of the places and people that you know from experience are your kryptonite. Make the list, pray over it, and establish a boundary you will not cross, lest you be exposed to spiritual danger.

"When we pray for the Spirit's help...we will simply fall down at the Lord's feet in our weakness. There we will find the victory and power that comes from His love." —ANDREW MURRAY

ESTABLISH THE PEACE
OF GOD IN YOUR LIFE

And the peace of God, which passeth all understanding, shall keep your hearts and minds through Christ Jesus (PHILIPPIANS 4:7).

If we have the peace of God, it will squelch all fears and worries. This remedy to life's roller-coaster circumstances is beyond human understanding—but then, we don't really need to understand it. We just need to establish the peace of God in our lives as if it were an anchor... which it is.

Trouble may raise its head today, but you can be prepared by knowing that God's peace will bring you through. Let it guard both your heart and your mind. You will be safe.

"Is the peace of God in the soul disturbed by things down here? No, never! If waters break in stormy currents against a rock, the rock is unmoved; it is only the waters that are disturbed."
—G.V. WIGRAM

Buyer's Remorse

Take heed therefore unto yourselves, and to all the flock, over the which the Holy Ghost hath made you overseers, to feed the church of God, which he hath purchased with his own blood (ACTS 20:28).

Did you ever buy something and later regret it? That's buyer's remorse. We may encounter it often in our lives, but God never has buyer's remorse. He has purchased us without regret, knowing ahead of time what the purchase involved: a high price (the blood of Christ) for our moth-eaten rags of human righteousness.

We may notice a friend pay a high price for an item we know is worthless and shake our heads in wonder. But when we consider God's "foolish" purchase, we can only rejoice that God always buys wisely, especially when we're the purchased ones.

"Safe! Yes! Will God part with the objects of His highest love? Never! Will Jesus surrender the purchase of His own heart's blood? Never! Happy! Yes; if anything can render us happy, this should: that we are God's choice and the Savior's purchase; that the Father and the Son jointly claim us, and highly value us!" —JAMES SMITH

Fulfilling the Law of Christ

Bear ye one another's burdens, and so fulfill the law of Christ (GALATIANS 6:2).

How does God meet the needs of His people? More often than not, the miracle comes *through* His people. In the book of Acts, we see a church where needs were met by believers voluntarily pooling their resources. Needs were seen and then needs were met.

How is it with us, twenty centuries later? No doubt in God's mind we're still to be the channel through which God's gifts flow. When we withdraw from meeting the needs of others, the channel is dammed up and needs remain unmet.

Every Christian man has the charge to care for others. In so doing, we fulfill the law of Christ.

"We all need each other. Not one of us could carry on without others to share his burdens. And we begin to be like Christ only when we begin to help others, to be of use to them, to make life a little easier for them, to give them some of our strength in their weakness, some of our joy in their sorrow. When we have learned this lesson we have begun to live worthily." —J.R. MILLER

CONSIDER WHAT GREAT THINGS

Only fear the LORD, and serve him in truth with all your heart: for consider how great things he hath done for you (1 SAMUEL 12:24).

Every Christian man has a past with the Lord. If a new believer, the past may be short; only weeks or months. For many men, their past spans the course of years or even decades. During that time—long or short—God has proven Himself faithful. Through trials galore, through temptations aplenty, through health and sickness, God has been there. Often, though, we pass on through life barely recalling the "great things" He has done.

God asks that we fear Him, serve Him, and consider our past with Him, recalling the miracles we've experienced. What miracle can you bring to mind today to rejoice over God's faithfulness?

"There is nothing good in my daily life but has come by His blessing and gift. There is no deliverance from danger, no sudden incoming of joy, no softening and mellowing and sanctifying through trial which He did not devise and send."
—ALEXANDER SMELLIE

GOD'S SUPPLY

When they were filled, he said unto his disciples, Gather up the fragments that remain, that nothing be lost (JOHN 6:12).

When we were children and were delighted by candy or a new toy, we might have said—or even demanded—"More! More!" But we're men now, no longer children. We learn from Scripture that God gives us enough. If we truly need more, God will multiply what we have—just as He did with the loaves and fishes. There is no scarcity with God. Let your needs be known to Him and watch for His perfect supply. It will be enough, with pieces left over.

"Have you been holding back from a risky, costly course to which you know in your heart God has called you? Hold back no longer. Your God is faithful to you, and adequate for you. You will never need more than He can supply, and what He supplies, both materially and spiritually, will always be enough for the present." —J.I. PACKER

HIDDEN IN CHRIST

Thou art my hiding place; thou shalt preserve me from trouble;thou shalt compass me about with songs of deliverance. Selah (PSALM 32:7).

During times of danger or just daily stress, God desires to be our hiding place. Here is where we are preserved from trouble. We are surrounded by songs of holy deliverance. Here we can be safe from temptation. Here the evil one cannot approach us. Here we rest and regain our strength for daily living. Here is where we live with God.

"All those who in time of danger are duly sensible of it, and make use of God as their refuge and hiding place shall find him to be that to them, which their faith expects from him."
—ROBERT LEIGHTON

HEALTHY AND WHOLE

Beloved, I wish above all things that thou mayest prosper and be in health, even as thy soul prospereth (3 JOHN 1:2).

As the apostle John prayed for the readers of his letter that all would go well with them, so too can we believe God desires for all to go well with us. Yes, there will be life's rough patches, but the secret is that when we are going through adversity, we keep walking until we come out on the other side. God's will leads us on to wholeness. It's not God's will for us to be living below the level of His perfect plan for each of us.

God desires us to be healthy and whole.

"These three things, so necessary to the comfort of life, every Christian may in a certain measure expect, and for them every Christian is authorized to pray; and we should have more of all three if we devoutly prayed for them." —ADAM CLARKE

TENDER MERCIES

Remember, O LORD, thy tender mercies and thy lovingkindnesses; for they have been ever of old (PSALM 25:6).

Many Christian men have a history that portrays God as less than merciful, not an example of loving-kindness. For these men, God was a hard taskmaster, and their performances were seemingly measured by God's yardstick and always came up short. What a miserable way to live. It's like the poor donkey who only moves ahead as he tries to catch up with the carrot on the string in front of him.

Blessed is the man who has discovered that God is full of tender mercies and offers at every turn the benefits of His loving-kindness. They are "of old" and yet never grow old. Daily we're invited to feast on His mercy and loving-kindness.

"It is the multitude of His mercies that makes Him so merciful a God. He does not give but a drop or two of mercy—that would soon be gone, like the rain which fell this morning under the hot sun. But His mercies flow like a river! There is in Him…a multitude of mercies, for a multitude of sins, and a multitude of sinners!" —J.C. PHILPOT

The Need to Forgive and Move On with Your Life

And when ye stand praying, forgive, if ye have ought against any: that your Father also which is in heaven may forgive you your trespasses (MARK 11:25).

Some Christian men…perhaps you…have suffered needlessly because of someone else's actions or words. These wounds are surely painful and, yes, God sees the hurt. But if there is unforgiveness due to ill-treatment, the pain will only linger and perhaps end up in bitterness. For our own sakes, God calls us to forgive others. It doesn't really matter if they see their part in an offense. If they will not or cannot be involved in righting a wrong, you must deal with it yourself.

Forgiveness brings us out of the rut we're in. It stops the tape from endlessly replaying the offense in our heads. Best of all, when we forgive, our heavenly Father is able to forgive us for our many trespasses.

"He that cannot forgive others, breaks the bridge over which he himself must pass if he would ever reach heaven; for everyone has need to be forgiven." —GEORGE HERBERT

The Mind of Christ

For who hath known the mind of the Lord, that he may instruct him? but we have the mind of Christ (1 Corinthians 2:16).

Need wisdom? Need an answer to a tough problem? If so, remember that we're not left to figure things out with our own human (and fallible) wisdom. We have the mind of Christ. We're able to think things through with godly reason. We can weigh our options against the Word of God.

Is one of our options questionable or inappropriate according to God's Word? If so, we have our answer. When the Bible doesn't give clear counsel, we can pray and ask God to reveal the right course—and then make that decision in faith. In some matters, it's wise to share your situation with a trusted Christian friend. Talking about it may reveal the answer. Never rush toward an answer. Give God time to reveal the correct path.

"True religion is having the mind of Christ."—John Angell James

FIRE IN OUR BOSOMS?

Can a man take fire in his bosom, and his clothes not be burned? (PROVERBS 6:27).

We Christian men can make a mess of things when we figuratively carry fire in our bosoms by flirting with temptation. During temptation, a false promise presents itself to us, and we must decide whether to believe this false promise and act on it or refuse to accept it, knowing both its source and its end. Many men have been severely burned by the fire in their bosoms when they fanned the flame with their consent to temptation. A wise man will quickly discern the kindling fire and put it out without a second thought. *No good thing can result from fire in a man's bosom.*

"The temptation once yielded to gains power. The crack in the embankment which lets a drop or two ooze through is soon a hole which lets out a flood." —ALEXANDER MACLAREN

ACCOUNTABILITY

*Obey them that have the rule over you, and submit yourselves:
for they watch for your souls, as they that must give account,
that they may do it with joy, and not with grief: for that is
unprofitable for you* (HEBREWS 13:17).

Accountability for many men is like having a parent
watching over you once again. And yet, God does
appoint people in the Bible and in the church to whom
we should be accountable without reluctance. Accountability is a blessing, not a curse.

Consider the many Christian men caught up in some
form of addiction. Such men often find an accountability partner essential to their recovery. What if those men
had a person to whom they were accountable *before* they
fell into addiction?

Every growing Christian man should desire to have
someone to whom he can be accountable. He should
also be available as someone to whom someone in need
can be accountable.

*"It is one of the severest tests of friendship to tell your friend his
faults. So to love a man that you cannot bear to see a stain
upon him, and to speak painful truth through loving words,
that is friendship."* —HENRY WARD BEECHER

Encouraging Ourselves
in the Lord

David was greatly distressed; for the people spake of stoning him, because the soul of all the people was grieved, every man for his sons and for his daughters: but David encouraged himself in the Lord his God (1 Samuel 30:6).

There are times when a man must face serious situations alone. No one is able to help. At such times it's up to that man to encourage himself in the Lord his God.

How so? One way is to resort to the encouragement found in God's Word. Find and meditate on Scriptures that bless you. Another way is to recall God's past faithfulness. Perhaps David encouraged himself by recalling his victory over Goliath. Or simply turning to praise is yet another way of encouraging ourselves in the Lord. No matter the situation, praise always lifts our burdens.

The bottom line is that in the alone times when we must be encouraged, we have the power to do so.

*"Encourage yourself in God. Whatever you lose, whatever you lack, He will supply all you need. All things in earth and Heaven are His, and if you trust in Him, no good thing will He withhold." —*George Everard

GOOD COUNSEL

Thy testimonies also are my delight and my counselors (PSALM 119:24).

No man is free from the need of counseling. Life often presents dilemmas that require wisdom beyond ourselves. In such situations, a man's first resort for counseling is God's Word. This is especially true if we have learned to *delight* in God's Word, knowing it will never lead us astray. God often allows circumstances that require us to lean hard on His Word.

It may come as no shock to think of the book of Proverbs as one of the fountains of wisdom in the Bible. With thirty-one chapters, many men have found it beneficial to read a chapter a day throughout the month and then begin again the next month. The wisdom of Solomon can help us in our present situations and caution us against the mistakes that require us to make hard choices or that will prompt repentance.

"If honest of heart and uprightness before God were lacking or if I did not patiently wait on God for instruction, or if I preferred the counsel of my fellow-men to the declarations of the Word of God, I made great mistakes." —GEORGE MÜLLER

SELF-ACCEPTANCE

I will praise thee; for I am fearfully and wonderfully made: marvelous are thy works; and that my soul knoweth right well (PSALM 139:14).

Few men are aware of their own giftedness. And yet we know every man *is* gifted by God. Every man is created in God's image and has been deemed of great value to God as evidenced by Christ's death on the cross. It seems strange then that some men devalue themselves or are unaware of their importance in God's unfolding will.

Some men find it hard to accept their lot in life, and yet for every man born from above, indwelt by God's Holy Spirit, there is great acceptance by God. How then can we who are the children of God question our worth? God has answered that question with total resolve. Self-esteem in every Christian man should be off the charts. We are accepted, acceptable, deeply loved, and deeply valued.

"The saints are God's jewels, highly esteemed by and dear to him; they are a royal diadem in his hand." —MATTHEW HENRY

It's All by Faith

For therein is the righteousness of God revealed from faith to faith: as it is written, The just shall live by faith (ROMANS 1:17).

The Christian life is begun by faith...and sustained through our whole lives by that same faith. Most of us learned fairly early that faith is the ever-present Miracle-Gro for our lives.

This faith is what began God's work in us, and it's by this faith that He will continue to perform the work until the day of Jesus Christ.

That means we continue to believe in God for our entire lives and all that pertains to them. We believed in God first for salvation, but then we also must go on believing in Him for our sustenance, our finances, our health, our relationships, our jobs...It all comes from His hand through faith. Even faith that carries us through the cloudy days when we can't really get a handle on what God's doing with us. Faith knows God has the handle. We'll be fine.

"Daily living by faith on Christ is what makes the difference between the sickly and the healthy Christian, between the defeated and the victorious saint." —A.W. PINK

Epistles to a
World of Lost Men

And the angel of the LORD appeared unto him, and said unto him, The LORD is with thee, thou mighty man of valour (JUDGES 6:12).

Are we a weakened generation of men? If so, we must consider that in our present weakness there is hidden great opportunity. For too long we have allowed our appetites to rule us. Have we not misused the gifts of God...or left them unused? Have not our sexual lives been more patterned after the world than patterned after God's plan for sexuality?

There are men who watch us as Christians, wondering if we truly have answers that could benefit them. Thus we are God's epistles to a world of lost men. But in order to reach them, we ourselves must be truly found. May no man within our circle of influence be lost without our witness being real to him.

"Soon we shall be up there with Christ. God did not mean us to be happy without Him; but God would first have us to be witnesses for Him down here, to hold out as much light as we can." —G.V. WIGRAM

The Equipping Comes
with the Calling

Wherefore I put thee in remembrance that thou stir up the gift of God, which is in thee by the putting on of my hands (2 TIMOTHY 1:6).

God is faithful in calling each of us to a specific work. And what we are called to do, we are equipped to do. For many men, fear or feelings of inadequacy keep them from stepping out and believing in God for an effective life.

A man's calling in life may be large or small, but it is never without the means to fulfill it. Prayer opens the door to our assignment, but we must move one step at a time toward our purpose. The result will be much fruit, and when our lives end, we will look back and be satisfied that we didn't miss out on the blessing of our personal calling in life.

"Next to faith this is the highest art—to be content with the calling in which God has placed you." —MARTIN LUTHER

The Depth of God's Love

But God commendeth his love toward us, in that, while we were yet sinners, Christ died for us (ROMANS 5:8).

Isn't it remarkable that God should love us so fully? Isn't it a miracle to be considered by God as valued enough to send His Son to die for us?

Truth be known, we may never fully grasp the depth of God's love in this lifetime. We can only marvel and give thanks.

We may think we're just one in eight billion that God loves—and that His love is diffused among the many. But no. God's love is focused on each of us. *Focused!* We exist to receive His love as if each of us was the only creation He loves. What manner of love is this!

"Believe God's love and power more than you believe your own feelings and experiences. Your rock is Christ, and it is not the rock that ebbs and flows but the sea." —SAMUEL RUTHERFORD

God's Timing Is Perfect

So teach us to number our days, that we may apply our hearts unto wisdom (PSALM 90:12).

If we were to plan the events in our lives, we would no doubt speed things up a bit. We don't like waiting, especially if it's for something we truly want. But God, not us, sets the timetable for our lives' events. And when He seems slow, we can know that "waiting on the Lord" is a valuable learning tool God loves to use. The Bible is full of men who waited. Noah waited. Moses waited. David waited. Joseph waited. Jacob waited. Even Jesus waited until the fullness of time. Let us, then, be patient and wait for God to bring to pass His promises.

"The prayer that begins with trustfulness, and passes on into waiting, will always end in thankfulness, triumph, and praise."—ALEXANDER MACLAREN

OUR INTERIOR VOICE

Bless the LORD, O my soul: and all that is within me, bless his holy name (PSALM 103:1).

Every man has an interior voice that speaks to him throughout the day. Much of what we say to ourselves relates to the mundane matters of life. But then every man has that voice that accuses him of not measuring up or of having failed in the past. Sometimes the voice provokes fear and anxiety. But when that voice starts to repeat the condemning or fearful tapes we've heard time and again, it's up to us to stop that voice and replace it by speaking affirming words to ourselves. David spoke to himself and benefited from his words. Each of us can do likewise. Today, when your interior voice starts to speak destructive thoughts, shut it down by speaking thoughts of faith and courage.

"Most unhappiness comes from listening to ourselves instead of talking to ourselves." —MARTYN LLOYD JONES

COMPARING OURSELVES
WITH OTHERS

For we dare not make ourselves of the number, or compare ourselves with some that commend themselves: but they measuring themselves by themselves, and comparing themselves among themselves, are not wise (2 CORINTHIANS 10:12).

It may bolster our self-esteem to compare ourselves positively with some other men who are not as successful, strong, handsome, or smart as we are. It may also bring us down to compare ourselves negatively with men who we may envy for their apparently happy lot. But in either case, we're on the wrong track. Measuring ourselves by comparison with others is not God's way. We are all unique men with distinct personalities, strengths, and weaknesses, and specific callings in life.

Be the man you know you're called to be. That will bring about contentment and the end of faulty comparisons.

"Men compare themselves with men, and readily with the worst, and flatter themselves with that comparative betterness. This is not the way to see spots, to look into the muddy streams of profane men's lives; but look into the clear fountain of the Word, and there we may both discern and wash them; and consider the infinite holiness of God, and this will humble us to the dust." —ROBERT LEIGHTON

WHERE DID GOD FIND YOU?

He found him in a desert land, and in the waste howling wilderness; he led him about, he instructed him, he kept him as the apple of his eye (DEUTERONOMY 32:10).

God's love for Israel is pictured as a man found by God in a desert land. God led him, instructed him, and kept him as the apple of His eye. In short, God found Israel in its great need—and He meant to fill that need. He still does that today...searching each of us out in our great need with the goal of leading us out of our personal desert, instructing us in life, and yes, keeping each of us as the apple of His eye.

Where did God find you when you first met Him? Was it in the desert? Or did the desert come later? Where does God find you today? Wherever you are, God is there to lead you out.

You are the apple of His eye.

"Christian! God has found you! God is leading you! God is instructing you! Oh, then, leave to Him to choose your path in life!" —JOHN MACDUFF

MISTAKES

The LORD will perfect that which concerneth me: thy mercy, O LORD, endureth for ever: forsake not the works of thine own hands (PSALM 138:8).

Every man makes mistakes. Some make many mistakes daily. But whether our mistakes are few or many, big or small, God has the power—and the will—to override our errors in such a way as to turn the situation around for our ultimate good, though that may not be seen immediately. Many a man's seeming mistake became the pivot God used to bring that man into a new place of blessing.

When you suffer from the effects of a wrong turn in life, let prayer and faith make that wrong turn a turn onto the perfect path of God's will. As a bonus, when we must suffer from the mistakes of another, God is also willing to turn that to our good. But faith and often patience are key. Don't be rattled when God is pivoting you into a new phase of life.

"We serve a gracious Master who knows how to overrule even our mistakes to His glory and our own advantage." —JOHN NEWTON

A Man's Limits

And he said unto them, Come ye yourselves apart into a desert place, and rest a while: for there were many coming and going, and they had no leisure so much as to eat (MARK 6:31).

Every man must know his limits and honor them. They are there to keep him safe. Stress is a huge killer of men, and that stress is often caused by men exceeding their capacity for work or some other activity that consumes time and energy.

We are built by God to be useful and to stay busy. But God has also set limits on what our bodies and brains can handle. Learn your limits the easy way—by marking how far you can go before anxiety sets in. Don't learn the hard way through deteriorating health or a meltdown.

Limits are your friends.

"Man's spiritual life consists in the number and fulness of his correspondences with God. In order to develop these he may be constrained to insulate them, to enclose them from the other correspondences, to shut himself in with them. In many ways the limitation of the natural life is the necessary condition of the full enjoyment of the spiritual life." —HENRY DRUMMOND

GOD HAS YOUR BACK

My little children, these things write I unto you, that ye sin not. And if any man sin, we have an advocate with the Father, Jesus Christ the righteous (1 JOHN 2:1).

One of the truest tests of commitment comes during hard times. Who has our back when we're under attack? Who will watch over us with true loyalty? Who will be in our corner when we mess up?

Only Christ. He is our permanent and loyal brother. He will never fail us…especially during those times when our earthly friends do.

What then is our response to this overwhelming loyalty? Isn't it that we return that loyalty to Christ? When He is under attack, do we speak up in His defense? Do we recommend Him to our acquaintances going through tough times? Loyalty should beget loyalty. And loyalty is based on commitment. Are we as fully committed to Christ today as He is to us?

"Faith does not grasp a doctrine, but a heart. The trust which Christ requires is the bond that unites souls with Him; and the very life of it is entire committal of myself to Him in all my relations and for all my needs, and absolute utter confidence in Him as all sufficient for everything that I can require."
—ALEXANDER MACLAREN

SIN IS LEAVEN

A little leaven leaveneth the whole lump (GALATIANS 5:9).

In the Bible, sin is likened to leaven. During the Passover, leaven was removed from the house as part of God's directive to keep the angel of death at bay. In the New Testament, the Lord's Table is celebrated with unleavened bread—typifying a renunciation of sin.

The analogy is fitting. Sin is like leaven in its ability to enlarge its place in our lives in the same way leaven enlarges the loaf. And doesn't a little sin often lead to additional sin? A pinch of sin, like leaven, expands easily; and if we give way to sin, sin becomes our master.

Let every man, then, remove the leaven of sin from his life. May every celebration of the Lord's Table remind us of the necessary absence of the leaven of sin in our lives.

"Little sins are very dangerous! A little leaven, leavens the whole lump. A little knife, may kill. A little leak in a ship, may sink it. Though the scorpion is little—yet will it sting a lion to death! Just so, a little sin may at once bar the door of Heaven, and open the gates of Hell!" —THOMAS BROOKS

A DIVINE NATURE

Whereby are given unto us exceeding great and precious promises: that by these ye might be partakers of the divine nature, having escaped the corruption that is in the world through lust (2 PETER 1:4).

In Christ we find not just a Savior from the dire penalty of sin but also a deliverer from the power of sin. At our conversion we were given a new nature that doesn't recognize the power of sin. Abiding in our new nature enables us to overcome the sins that cause us to fall prey to our "old man."

True, we may not always *feel* as though we have a new nature, but then, there's no place in the Bible where we are told to reckon according to our feelings.

Today and always, live according to God's promises, and reckon yourself alive by virtue of your new nature.

"If we had the tongue of the mightiest of orators, and if that tongue could be touched with a live coal from off the altar, yet still it could not utter a tenth of the praises of the exceeding great and precious promises of God." —CHARLES SPURGEON

THE SCULPTING OF GOD

It is God that girdeth me with strength, and maketh my way perfect (PSALM 18:32).

Left to ourselves, we might design our lives differently from the way God has designed them. We would certainly allow for less sorrow, fewer run-ins with sin, and a more carefree existence. But when we realize that God is always doing something behind the scenes of our circumstances, we can bear the ups and downs of life more easily.

Every seeming adversity has its redemption when accepted by faith as God's tool for sculpting us into the image of Christ. Praise God for life's happy times, but praise Him also during the valleys. It's there that we truly grow as we learn submission to the sculpting of God.

"The divine Sculptor must do with us, as the sculptor did with the stone. He must bring to bear upon us the sharp chisel of affliction, of disappointment, of trial. It seems that these things will destroy us...But all the time, the Master Sculptor with His sharp chisel of pain, is only carving His own image in their natures and characters." —CHARLES NAYLOR

Our Limited Vision

O Lord God, thou hast begun to show thy servant thy greatness, and thy mighty hand: for what God is there in heaven or in earth, that can do according to thy works, and according to thy might? (Deuteronomy 3:24).

We men often have such limited vision when it comes to who we are. Especially who we are in Christ. God simply doesn't make second-rate men. Every man has more potential than he'll ever use. Of course, this man knows well enough that his potential comes from God, not from any merit of his own. And seldom do we really comprehend the power of God when it comes to animating our own lives. When it gets down to it, we men are more than we think we are because our God is more than we think He is.

"If a Christian remains in a carnal condition long after experiencing new birth, he hinders God's salvation from realizing its full potential and manifestation. Only when he is growing in grace, constantly governed by the spirit, can salvation be wrought in him."—Watchman Nee

LIFE TO THE HILT

A wise man is strong; yea, a man of knowledge increaseth strength (PROVERBS 24:5).

Jim Elliot lived a short life of twenty-nine years…but he lived it to the hilt and died a martyr for Christ. The tribe he had hoped to reach for Christ became his murderers. But that wasn't the end of the story. Eventually, many of those who killed Jim became followers of Christ. His influence continues today through the story of his life as written by his widow, Elisabeth Elliot. If we could talk to Jim and tell him how sorry we are for his tragic end, he would surely tell us not to waste our tears—that he did indeed live his life to the hilt by fulfilling God's purpose in his death.

We're not likely to have the same calling as Jim Elliot, but whatever our calling and however short or long our earthly lives, we can and must live them to the hilt. Anything less is an insult to God—the one who desires us to be all there, wherever we find ourselves.

"Wherever you are, be all there. Live to the hilt every situation you believe to be the will of God." —JIM ELLIOT

God's Investment

Thou oughtest therefore to have put my money to the exchangers, and then at my coming I should have received mine own with usury (MATTHEW 25:27).

God has something invested in you, and He will not let that investment fail to yield its dividends. What, though, do we have invested in God? Are they eternal investments? Will there be generous dividends? Or will our investments fail to yield a profit?

Just as God has invested in us, so too must we invest in Him. We do this by *daily* responding to the gospel afresh, anticipating another day of profit.

Our response may be that of prayer, it might mean a literal financial investment with someone in need, or it might mean laying down our lives in some meaningful way that brings benefit to another person. Count on it: There will be a way to invest in God today.

"It is the very essence of true religion, to feel that God is ours. To have him for our portion, yields the highest comfort, and invests with the greatest wealth in time and in eternity."
—WILLIAM NICHOLSON

GIVE DILIGENCE

Wherefore the rather, brethren, give diligence to make your calling and election sure: for if ye do these things, ye shall never fall (2 PETER 1:10).

E very man has a distinct calling. But by calling, we don't need to think of heading off to seminary or the mission field (unless that is indeed God's calling for you). A laborer, a teacher, a banker, a store manager, a cement mason—no matter the label we put on our day's work, it can be as important a calling as Billy Graham's. Why? Because it's *our* calling, and it will use our talents, strength, and time to the best advantage. So let us be bold in our day's work, whatever it is. And if we can't be bold and confident in our calling, maybe we should ask ourselves, *Is this indeed my calling?*

"Take care of giving up your first zeal; beware of cooling in the least degree. Ye were hot and earnest once; be hot and earnest still, and let the fire which once burnt within you still animate you. Be ye still men of might and vigour, men who serve their God with diligence and zeal."—CHARLES SPURGEON

A MAN AND HIS BROTHERS

Two are better than one; because they have a good reward for their labor. For if they fall, the one will lift up his fellow: but woe to him that is alone when he falleth; for he hath not another to help him up (ECCLESIASTES 4:9-10).

Our culture likes to portray genuine manhood as the rugged "can-do-anything" individualist attitude. But for Christian men, we understand the power of our brotherhood with other believers. We are not complete in ourselves; we need the rest of the Body of Christ, particularly our brothers in Christ. Often our inadequacies can be filled by the strengths in other men, just as we may supply our strengths to complete a brother's weakness.

Brotherhood is by God's design. Friendship is God's gift to men. Don't go alone in life. Bring your brothers along. The pleasures of the journey will be multiplied when shared with other men.

"There is a brotherhood within the body of believers, and the Lord Jesus Christ is the common denominator. Friendship and fellowship are the legal tender among believers."
—J. VERNON MCGEE

BIBLICAL PRINCIPLES

But this I say, He which soweth sparingly shall reap also sparingly; and he which soweth bountifully shall reap also bountifully (2 CORINTHIANS 9:6).

The Bible is more than a revelation of God and His kingdom. In its pages we're given various principles that when followed will enhance our likelihood of success. Every major life event—marriage, vocation, finances, parenting—and even manhood itself will be safeguarded as we obey what God's Word tells us. When we neglect godly principles, we venture into dangerous territory.

We may find broken relationships, financial loss, parenting failures, and health problems in the wake of our disobedience of God's Word. But even then, one of God's principles involves restoration when we have exceeded the boundaries of Scripture. If one or more areas of your life are suffering due to a violation of a biblical principle, search out in God's Word the violation and its remedy. As you reintroduce the principle in your life, give God time to bring about healing. Like a seed planted, your restoration will sprout and grow like a mighty oak.

"The safe place lies in obedience to God's Word, singleness of heart and holy vigilance." —A.B. SIMPSON

Open the Gift That
Is Your Future

These things I have spoken unto you, that in me ye might have peace. In the world ye shall have tribulation: but be of good cheer; I have overcome the world (JOHN 16:33).

We live in perilous times. There can be great cause for fear among men who will not trust in God, but to be a Christian man is to expect a blessed future. We look forward to success, not failure. We seek and receive favor from God in our endeavors. When the headlines report dire circumstances, we know to exalt God's Word above the latest prediction. Trouble may come through financial reverses, scarcity of resources, weather-related events, or personal setbacks. But in every case, God sees and God provides. We must never give in to fear in the light of world events. Trust in God for both small and large changes.

"Faith, which is trust, and fear are opposite poles. If a man has the one, he can scarcely have the other in vigorous operation. He that has his trust set upon God does not need to dread anything except the weakening or the paralyzing of that trust."
—ALEXANDER MACLAREN

The God Who Is Needy

Verily I say unto you, Inasmuch as ye have done it unto one of the least of these my brethren, ye have done it unto me (MATTHEW 25:40).

It's odd to imagine God being needy. And yet Jesus tells us that as we tend to the needy, we're tending to Him. In short, God cares for people through each of us. Thus the needs of others are the needs of God.

If we want to see God while on this earth, we can see Him in the faces of the lonely, the sick, and the poor. And when we tend to the needs of God by helping others (irony of all ironies), we're more blessed than those to whom we give.

If every Christian man would tend to the needs of those around him, what an impact it would make on the unbelieving world.

"Giving of alms is a glorious work, and let me assure you it is not unfruitful work. Whatever is disbursed to the poor brethren, is given to Christ!... The poor man's hand is Christ's treasury, and there is nothing lost that is put there." —THOMAS WATSON

GOD IS THE DAD
YOU NEVER HAD

We have had fathers of our flesh which corrected us, and we gave them reverence: shall we not much rather be in subjection unto the Father of spirits, and live? (HEBREWS 12:9).

How was it with your dad? Was he a good or even great dad? Or was there something missing from your paternal relationship? For many men, there was no dad on the scene. For others, Dad was physically present but emotionally absent. If your dad was missing in action, you can know that God is the dad you never had.

As adult men, we forgive our less-than-perfect dads and transfer our primary allegiance to our heavenly dad. If our father on earth is or was a good dad, his attributes should point us to the One who exhibits those attributes in full measure.

Whether your relationship with your dad was good, poor, or nonexistent, you can now trust in the true father of us all.

"God is the archetypal Father; all other fatherhood is a more or less imperfect copy of his perfect fatherhood." —F.F. BRUCE

THE DISCORDANT NOTE

Speaking to yourselves in psalms and hymns and spiritual songs, singing and making melody in your heart to the Lord (EPHESIANS 5:19).

My friend plays the guitar as he leads worship in our church. One day he said, "If I make a mistake as I'm playing, I have to go on. If I keep thinking about the mistake I made a measure ago, I can't play the music."

There's a lesson there. We're all making music with our lives. And when we've hit the wrong note, we have to let it go and play the present notes. There's no recapturing a wrong note once played.

If your life's symphony has hit some wrong notes, keep playing your music and forget the discordant life behind you. The music in the next measure is up. Play it.

"It is with life as with music. The rests on the staff in one sense are not part of the music...yet they're as important...as if they were notes to be struck or sung... There are rests in life which are quite as important in the melody of life, as any notes on the staff. To overlook them...is to mar the music. We should mind the rests."—J.R. MILLER

Be Sure of God

And we know that all things work together for good to them that love God, to them who are the called according to his purpose (Romans 8:28).

As Christian men, we naturally believe in the existence of God. But is that enough to get us through? No, it isn't. To really get the most out of our Christian lives, we must be as certain of His goodness, His promises, His moment-by-moment presence as we are of His existence.

The whole of our lives can be spent happily becoming more and more certain of God each day. When trials come, we can be sure God sees and is active in resolving our situation. When we're in a season of blessing, we can know God is the source of that blessing. Being sure of God in every aspect of life bolsters our confidence that no matter what happens, everything will turn out for the best.

"We must learn to live on the heavenly side and look at things from above. To contemplate all things as God sees them, as Christ beholds them, overcomes sin, defies Satan, dissolves perplexities, lifts us above trials, separates us from the world and conquers fear of death." —A.B. Simpson

FORKS IN THE ROAD

Show me thy ways, O LORD; teach me thy paths (PSALM 25:4).

Every man is often faced with serious decisions, some of which could alter his life forever. How then to decide which fork in the road to take? Poet Robert Frost would tell us to take the path less traveled. And sometimes that is the best choice. But we can't reduce our decision-making to such a simplistic tactic. Instead, for the Christian man, there are barometers that can nudge us toward the right path. First, any decision must be supported by Scripture. Another test is to ask, Do those who know me best have an objective opinion? Then ask, Do the circumstances lead in one direction over another? Finally, we can trust our own God-given inner instincts (not to be confused with emotional influence) by asking, How do we truly feel about the choices?

In the final analysis, make all your decisions by faith. You'll never go wrong.

"It is the characteristic excellence of the strong man that he can bring momentous issues to the fore and make a decision about them. The weak are always forced to decide between alternatives they have not chosen themselves." —DIETRICH BONHOEFFER

A MAN'S TONGUE

If any man among you seem to be religious, and bridleth not his tongue, but deceiveth his own heart, this man's religion is vain (JAMES 1:26).

Whoso keepeth his mouth and his tongue keepeth his soul from troubles (PROVERBS 21:23).

Face it, for many Christian men, our tongues often betray us before we can formulate the most appropriate words to say. Anger, oversensitivity, and disappointment often result in harsh words that can't change our circumstances or even our mood. Instead, the situation is often made worse. If we would like to avoid troubles today, let's take a lesson from Solomon's playbook of Proverbs and "keepeth" our tongues, and thus our souls, from trouble. Choose to speak good words today, even if in the midst of adversity or turmoil.

"O Lord, keep our hearts, keep our eyes, keep our feet, and keep our tongues." —WILLIAM TIPTAFT

THE BOOK OF MY LIFE

Thou tellest my wanderings: put thou my tears into thy bottle: are they not in thy book? (PSALM 56:8).

Your life is like a book God has written just for you. Each day is the next page in the story, and you keep turning the pages, day by day, page by page, to see what happens next. You keep reading, too, to find out if the book of your life is a drama, comedy, or tragedy. Eventually, you realize it's a little of all three, measured out by God's timetable. And for every Christian man, no matter the measure of sadness or gladness in this life, the book of his life has a very happy ending.

"Every man is an original and solitary character. None can either understand or feel the book of his own life like himself."
—RICHARD CECIL

BUILDING A TOXIC
ENVIRONMENT FOR SATAN

Be sober, be vigilant; because your adversary the devil, as a roaring lion, walketh about, seeking whom he may devour (1 PETER 5:8).

Is your life toxic? It should be. Toxic, that is, to Satan. Some men mistakenly give little credence to the craftiness of our ruthless enemy and thus allow him unfettered influence in their lives. But wise Christian men not only refuse Satan any influence in their lives; they build safeguards that repel Satan. These safeguards are toxic to Satan, and he no longer assails the man whose very presence threatens him. Do not belittle your enemy. Be wise in keeping yourself from his clutches. Make your life toxic to the enemy.

"Satan trembles when he sees the weakest saint upon their knees." —WILLIAM COWPER

GOD IS AT WORK

Being confident of this very thing, that he which hath begun a good work in you will perform it until the day of Jesus Christ (PHILIPPIANS 1:6).

God is actively (not passively) at work in the life of every believing man. Our daily thoughts may for a brief while not include God, but God's thoughts of us and all that concerns us never cease. As you read these words, God, your Father, is performing the work of maturation in you and will do so for the rest of your life. And the work He performs, as Paul tells us, is a *good* work. When this realization becomes firmly affixed in our minds, we may be confident in all that God does in us and for us. Even as we read these words, His plans are moving us forward, never backward.

"The work of grace is but begun and carried on in this life—it is not finished here—it is not perfect here. As long as we are in this imperfect state, there is still something more to be done. We shall always find cause to go forward, to grow, to increase, to abound more and more." —WILLIAM NICHOLSON

A Shining Lamp

Thy word is a lamp unto my feet, and a light unto my path (Psalm 119:105).

The Bible isn't a textbook. Nor is it a theology thesis. For the Christian man, the Bible is a lamp shining on his path. No man really knows what his future holds. Will there be joys? Yes. Will there be trials? Of course. But in every circumstance, God illuminates a path only seen by the light of His Word. When we neglect or disobey the Word, we're prone to walking off the lighted path. But when we stay on the lighted path and follow where it leads, we will come through just fine.

Read the Word, certainly. But more than reading it, we must follow the path it illuminates for us.

"One who carries a lantern on a country-road at night, sees only one step before him. If he takes that step, he carries his lantern forward, and thus makes another step plain. At length he reaches his destination in safety, without once stepping into darkness. The whole way has been made light for him, though only a single step of it at a time. This illustrates the usual method of God's guidance." —J.R. Miller

REPENTANCE

Despisest thou the riches of his goodness and forbearance and longsuffering; not knowing that the goodness of God leadeth thee to repentance? (ROMANS 2:4).

What causes a man to repent? Regret plays a part. So does the conviction of the Holy Spirit. But Paul reminds us that one strong motivation for repentance is the goodness of God.

While some people will always carry a grudge against those who offended them, God isn't like that. Instead, God is like the father of the Prodigal Son. He eagerly yearned for the repentant son—and as the lad returned, the father welcomed him home. Not a word of reproach came from the father, though the son expected it. Such unwarranted goodness had to bring a sigh of relief to the son who hoped for no more than to be taken on by his father as a hired hand. A party was out of the question—and yet a party was on the father's mind.

When we have something from which we need to repent, let's remember that the goodness of God is waiting to accept our repentance by throwing a party.

"The goodness of God is a spiritual sunbeam to melt the heart into tears."—THOMAS WATSON

Pray, Lest You Become Prey

For the eyes of the Lord are over the righteous, and his ears are open unto their prayers: but the face of the Lord is against them that do evil (1 Peter 3:12).

Prayer is many things, but one of the most vital is its function as a spiritual weapon against the forces of evil. In the hour of great need, there is prayer. In the hour of temptation, there is prayer. In the hour of financial reverses, there is prayer. Relationship problems? Pray! Health issues? Pray! Even before all these and other dire situations arise, prayer is the wall that keeps the enemy without. Every man is called to pray and pray hardily. There are no exceptions.

Never let prayer become plan B, nor should prayer be a matter of neglect. As the old saying goes, seven days without prayer makes one weak.

"Oh, how strenuous is life! I know a little of it...How fierce the battle! I know something of the conflict, but I ought not to faint, because I can pray." —G. Campbell Morgan

God's Time

Humble yourselves therefore under the mighty hand of God, that he may exalt you in due time (1 PETER 5:6).

It's a fact that spiritual growth takes time. There are no instantly mature Christians. And those who claim to be so will find their roots shallow and likely will wither away in a short time. True Christian men know that the measure required to grow strong like a mighty oak takes time. Even years. And such men, though seemingly content with the time factor, know that as they wait, they must water their spiritual life with the Word. They know prayer sends down strong roots. Adversity builds muscle. Fellowship and community with other believers bring comfort and encouragement. The secret to growth isn't rocket science. Follow what you know you should do, and wait and watch. Growth always comes to those who seek it.

"He who waits on God loses no time." —VANCE HAVNER

Our Divine Helper

So that we may boldly say, The Lord is my helper, and I will not fear what man shall do unto me (HEBREWS 13:6).

One of the functions of the Holy Spirit is to be our divine Helper. One way He helps is to guide us into the right paths and detour us around the wrong ones. But for this to happen, we must develop the habit of listening. The boundaries the Holy Spirit establishes for us are divinely ordered and are given for our safety. The Holy Spirit speaks to us through the Word and occasionally through our spirit. But in the latter case, it will always be in accordance with the Word of God. The Holy Spirit never leads us in a way that contradicts what the Bible teaches.

Learn to listen today. Is God speaking through His Word, through prayer, through others you encounter? Are there boundaries the Holy Spirit has established for you that you have ignored or violated? Get back on the right path today, and trust the leading of the Holy Spirit.

"Faith never knows where it is being led, but it loves and knows the One who is leading." —OSWALD CHAMBERS

WEAKNESS IS STRENGTH

Therefore I take pleasure in infirmities, in reproaches, in necessities, in persecutions, in distresses for Christ's sake: for when I am weak, then am I strong (2 CORINTHIANS 12:10).

When circumstances shed light on our weaknesses, we can rejoice that the same light will also shed the light of God's strength. It's easy to defend ourselves or complain about a weakness revealed, but admitting weakness opens the door for God to move in strength.

What weakness is being revealed in you? Can you see this as an opportunity for God to enter into your weakness with His power and might? Weakness is never meant to embarrass us or make us feel less than. From God's perspective, the revelation of weakness is a good and necessary thing.

"Real true faith is man's weakness leaning on God's strength."
—D.L. MOODY

YOUR SPIRITUAL FOOTPRINT

For even hereunto were ye called: because Christ also suffered for us, leaving us an example, that ye should follow his steps (1 PETER 2:21).

Much is being said these days about the size of our carbon footprint. Are we careless with our use of energy and natural resources? That's a valid question, but more importantly, are we careless with our spiritual footprint?

There will always be new generations of young men coming up behind us, looking at the spiritual footprints we've left behind. What will they see? What will they say? Is our spiritual footprint worthy of someone else's steps? Can future generations look to what we've left behind and walk as we've walked?

Today and every day, we leave yet another print as we walk through our lives. Make today's footprint worthy of emulation.

"A Christian should be both a magnet and a diamond! A magnet in drawing others to Christ; a diamond in casting a sparkling luster of holiness, in his life. Oh let us be…so just in our dealings, so true in our promises, so devout in our worship, so unblamable in our lives; that we may be the walking pictures of Christ!" —THOMAS WATSON

CELEBRATING FAILURE

For a just man falleth seven times, and riseth up again: but the wicked shall fall into mischief (PROVERBS 24:16).

When we succeed, it's fun to celebrate our successes. But what do we do when we fail at something? It may be hard to do, but perhaps we should celebrate our failures too. Every failure has within it the seeds of wisdom. We probably learn more from failure than from success. The one thing we mustn't do in the light of failure is beat ourselves up over it. If we let it, the tape of accusation will loop over and over in our minds endlessly, bringing with it the useless and counterproductive guilt that can paralyze us from future attempts at success.

Celebrate success, but find a way to commemorate failure too.

"God may allow His servant to succeed when He has disciplined him to a point where he does not need to succeed to be happy. The man who is elated by success and is cast down by failure is still a carnal man. At best his fruit will have a worm in it." —A.W. TOZER

Remembering

After the same manner also he took the cup, when he had supped, saying, this cup is the new testament in my blood: this do ye, as oft as ye drink it, in remembrance of me (1 Corinthians 11:25).

An important part of Christians coming together is for remembrance. When Christians gather together to partake of Communion (the Lord's Supper in some churches), we're asked by Jesus to "remember." Remembering, for the Christian man, is a means of affirming over and over the reality behind the taking of the bread and the cup.

As a man ages, he has more and more of the Lord's work in his life to remember. Slowing our lives down so we actually take time to remember the Lord and what He's done is crucial. Today, call to mind some of God's greatest blessings in your life. Where has He brought you from and where is He taking you? Then the next time your fellowship enjoys the Lord's Supper, make sure to remember Him. Remember all His goodness to you.

"Memory is the treasure house of the mind wherein the monuments thereof are kept and preserved." —Thomas Fuller

A CHANNEL OF BLESSING

Give, and it shall be given unto you; good measure, pressed down, and shaken together, and running over, shall men give into your bosom. For with the same measure that ye mete withal it shall be measured to you again (LUKE 6:38).

Some Christian men seem gifted to become financially successful. Others, not so much. Their gifts lie elsewhere. But what are we to do with our gifts, whether they be large or small? The clear answer is that we're to pass on our blessings to others. If we have the gift of finances, we can surely voluntarily share with those in need. If our gifts are as simple as listening ears, those too can be put to good use. Virtually every gift God gives to man is meant to be shared. We're to become channels of God's blessings to others. Today identify a gift you have and figure out how you might pass it on to someone who needs it.

"Every good gift that we have had from the cradle up has come from God. If a man just stops to think what he has to praise God for, he will find there is enough to keep him singing praises for a week."—D.L. MOODY

LIFE AS A SERIES OF MIRACLES

For whoso findeth me findeth life, and shall obtain favor of the LORD (PROVERBS 8:35).

Through happy times and sad times, through the highs of life and the lows, life itself is a series of miracles. Every man's presence on earth is the first miracle of existence. Then day by day as life unfolds, so do the everyday miracles that make up a man's life. True, these miracles are best identified as a man ages. But even younger men can pause and take notice of the work of God in their lives so far. A man's conversion to Christ is the greatest miracle, but in most cases, surely not the last. To truly appreciate the daily miracles, we need to watch for them. Though some may be smaller than others and harder to notice, they are still there. If nothing else, consider that every breath you take today is a miracle. A wise friend once said, "You're alive, so live!" That's the best way to experience today's miracle.

"A Christian is a perpetual miracle." —CHARLES SPURGEON

AMBASSADORS FOR CHRIST

We are ambassadors for Christ, as though God did beseech you by us: we pray you in Christ's stead, be ye reconciled to God (2 CORINTHIANS 5:20).

Every Christian man has a story. Whether converted as a child, a teen, or an adult, a man's testimony is one of his greatest assets. But like any asset, a man's story must be invested. Paul referred to us as ambassadors for Christ, and so we are. When appropriate times to share our stories present themselves—often divinely appointed by God—we should speak of Christ in the same way an ambassador speaks of his home country. Our home country is heaven, but though we enter heaven upon our death, it's fair to say we inherit eternal life the moment we say yes to Christ. We become citizens of heaven though we are not yet residents of heaven. How we each came to Christ is a story we should rehearse in our minds frequently and be prepared to share with ease and conviction. Watch for such moments. Just make sure your testimony rings true to those who are observing your life.

"If lips and life do not agree, the testimony will not amount to much." —HARRY IRONSIDE

The Promises Must Be Believed

And this is the promise that he hath promised us, even eternal life (1 John 2:25).

Ours is a life built on the promises of God. When we're doubtful about our future, we can know God has already secured it, both here and in eternity. When faced with adversity, we can claim various promises of God. When tempted, we must lay a firm hold on the promises of God.

We must be strong in the Lord, knowing "He will not allow you to be tempted above that you are able to bear." "With the temptation he will provide a way of escape." The promises, when believed, are fatal to Satan's suggestions. "My grace is sufficient for you" rendered harmless all the buffetings of Satan in the case of Paul. Know God's Word. Beware of ignorance.

"Prayer, like faith, obtains promises, enlarges their operation, and adds to the measure of their results." —E.M. Bounds

SEARCH OUT THE PROMISES

Let us hold fast the profession of our faith without wavering; (for he is faithful that promised) (HEBREWS 10:23).

God is more aware of His promises to us than we are. He has them memorized while we yet seek them out, one by one. And the search for God's promises is a lifelong pursuit. We never run out of the need for the secure promises of God, and the promises never have an expiration date. God delights in our ongoing search for and faith in His promises. If you wish to delight God today, identify a need in your life and find the corresponding promises to claim.

"To believe that He will preserve us is, indeed, a means of preservation. God will certainly preserve us, and make a way of escape for us out of the temptation, should we fall. We are to pray for what God has already promised. Our requests are to be regulated by His promises and commands. Faith embraces the promises and so finds relief." —JOHN OWEN

Our Last Enemy

The last enemy that shall be destroyed is death (1 CORINTHIANS 15:26).

Every Christian man will eventually face death. How he handles the coming end of his days is important. First, he must set aside all fear. The sting of death is removed for the believer. Second, he must leave the timing of his departure to God. Third, all practical matters must be settled so he leaves no unwieldy burden to his loved ones.

If you think it's too early to think about death, the reality is that it's never too early to be ready. We may rightly wish for many more years of service. We may pray, like Jesus, for the cup to pass from us. But also like Jesus, we must finally acknowledge, "Not my will, but yours be done."

"Take care of your life and the Lord will take care of your death." —GEORGE WHITEFIELD

SELF-WORTH

If ye fulfil the royal law according to the scripture, Thou shalt love thy neighbor as thyself, ye do well (JAMES 2:8).

Some Christian men fall prey to the enemy's attacks that lead to low self-worth. It may come from an abusive childhood, broken relationships, vocational failure, health crises, or some other genesis. But God's love of each of us as manifested in His creating us should spur us on to proper self-worth and also enable us to truly love one another. It ends all comparisons with others and all competition to best our brother in Christ.

Today, give thanks to God for *you*. Do not accept any suggestions that you are less than. You're *more than* in God's eyes.

"There is a self-love which is corrupt, and the root of the greatest sins, and it must be put off and mortified; but there is a self-love which is the rule of the greatest duty: we must have a due concern for the welfare of our own souls and bodies." — MATTHEW HENRY

Our Shortcomings

Let your conversation be without covetousness; and be content with such things as ye have: for he hath said, I will never leave thee, nor forsake thee (HEBREWS 13:5).

What a mixture is every man! Part warrior, part thinker, part planner, part doer—and so much more. We're often partly successful and...often partly *un*successful. When the latter is our lot, we must remember that God's presence within us always trumps our many shortcomings. Focusing on our lacks—and every man has them—can only bring us down. Trusting God to fill in the many spaces we lack takes away the burden of "performance." We are who we are, shortcomings and all, and God is good with that—and so must we be.

"O slow of heart to believe and trust in the constant presence and overruling agency of our almighty Savior!" —ADONIRAM JUDSON

SPIRIT AND LIFE

It is the spirit that quickeneth; the flesh profiteth nothing: the words that I speak unto you, they are spirit, and they are life (JOHN 6:63).

What do we see when we read the Bible? Words on a page? Ink on paper? Yes, that's what we see on the surface, but if we mix what we read with faith, we find life in those words of Scripture. As we feed on the Word, we feed on life itself—spiritual life. As we meditate on the day's reading of Scripture, we internalize the very Word of God. We then find that being filled with the written Word of God is a giant step toward being filled with the Living Word. As the apostle John wrote in recording Jesus's words, we find spirit and life in the words of Christ. And as every man has learned, the flesh is, indeed, no help at all.

"The Bible is alive…it speaks to me…it has feet, it runs after me…it has hands, it lays hold of me." —MARTIN LUTHER

LEANING IN

The wicked flee when no man pursueth: but the righteous are bold as a lion (PROVERBS 28:1).

Increasingly we are leaning into a fallen world that accepts and even enjoys the corruption that comes with sin. But Christian men play an important role in holding back the forces of evil. To do so, we must lean into personal righteousness. We must cleave to that which is good and rebel against all that is evil. Silence and apathy aren't options. Prayer warriors must fall on their knees. Leaders must lead in righteousness. Compassion must be our badge as we become first responders to those hurt by sin and corruption.

If we listen hard, we can hear the cries of the captives and the victims of a fallen humanity. We hear the call of God to come alongside those who hurt. We must not flee from our responsibility; we must be as bold as lions.

"What does love look like? It has the hands to help others. It has the feet to hasten to the poor and needy. It has eyes to see misery and want. It has the ears to hear the sighs and sorrows of men. That is what love looks like." —AUGUSTINE

DUTY

He hath showed thee, O man, what is good; and what doth the LORD require of thee, but to do justly, and to love mercy, and to walk humbly with thy God? (MICAH 6:8).

A Christian must quickly discern his duty while here on earth. Duty to God, to self, to family, to church, to country, to his brothers and sisters in Christ. Duty, in fact, is the railroad track of God's will for us. When we find and assume our duties on our shoulders, we discover they automatically broaden to accommodate the weight of the new responsibilities. When Christian men abscond from their duties, they leave a hole they alone can fill. When we find our duties here on earth, we will discover that their geneses are simply to do justly, love mercy, and walk humbly with our God.

"The soldier is summoned to a life of active duty and so is the Christian." —WILLIAM GURNALL

BEING COUNTERCULTURAL

Beware lest any man spoil you through philosophy and vain deceit, after the tradition of men, after the rudiments of the world, and not after Christ (COLOSSIANS 2:8).

This present time is crying out for Christian men to be thoroughly Christian and thoroughly countercultural. Sunday Christians won't do in a society that is increasingly hostile to Christianity. The time to "go along to get along" is long past. Men must step up to the plate at home, in the workplace, and in the church.

God is seeking such men today. Men who refuse to be swayed by the latest emerging trends that continue to lower the standard that is manhood.

Even today may present a temptation to go along with the crowd. But the time to prepare to take a stand is before the pressure to cave presents itself.

Today, be thoroughly Christian. Tomorrow too.

"Manhood is made in the field of struggle and hardship, not in ways of ease and luxury. Hindrances are opportunities. Difficulty is a school for manhood. Strength is the glory of manhood." —J.R. MILLER

ORDER OUT OF CHAOS

By him were all things created, that are in heaven, and that are in earth, visible and invisible, whether they be thrones, or dominions, or principalities, or powers: all things were created by him, and for him: And he is before all things, and by him all things consist (COLOSSIANS 1:16-17).

It's man's privilege to—like God in whose image he is created—bring order out of chaos. Many men spend their lives in jobs bringing order into being. Others have hobbies requiring the often slow talent of bringing beauty and order into existence where there was previously disorder. A stump of wood under the carver's hand becomes an object of art. A composer takes the twelve notes of music and produces a symphony. A house painter brings restoration to the chaos of a dilapidated fixer-upper. A wise counselor helps a tormented soul sort out the causes of his mental disorder.

What sorts of chaos in your life can you work to bring about order to? When you do, you're engaged in God's work.

"The Spirit brings order out of chaos and beauty out of ugliness. He can transform a sin-blistered man into a paragon of virtue. The Spirit changes people." —R.C. SPROUL

PRAYER IS NOT
WISHING ON STEROIDS

I exhort therefore, that, first of all, supplications, prayers, inter-cessions, and giving of thanks, be made for all men (1 TIM-OTHY 2:1).

When tragedy happens, we hear the call for "thoughts and prayers." And yes, prayer is certainly called for. But are our prayers simply thoughts that reach no higher than the ceiling? A Christian man is by necessity a praying man. He prays with genuine concern for those he intercedes for. His prayers are not mere thoughts, nor are they simply wishes for a happy outcome.

Today's Christian man knows the furtherance of God's will is influenced by his prayers. He prays boldly. He prays with faith. He prays with clarity. And God hears and answers that man's prayers.

"The more praying there is in the world, the better the world will be; the mightier the forces against evil everywhere."
—E.M. BOUNDS

MOVING FORWARD

Without faith it is impossible to please him: for he that cometh to God must believe that he is, and that he is a rewarder of them that diligently seek him (HEBREWS 11:6).

The Christian life isn't a static life. We never stand still in our growth in Christ. Rather, from day to day, week to week, year to year, we move forward in our walk with the Lord. We come upon stumbling blocks and walk past them. We go through dark tunnels and emerge into the light. We take a misstep backward but then take two recovery steps forward.

God never stops tending to our growth. He sets in motion the very circumstances we need to move ahead. Nothing can stop us from growing, for we are Christian men.

"The Christian life is very much like climbing a hill of ice. You cannot slide up. You have to cut every step with an ice axe. Only with incessant labor in cutting and chipping can you make any progress. If you want to know how to backslide, leave off going forward. Cease going upward and you will go downward of necessity. You can never stand still."
—CHARLES SPURGEON

LIFE MANAGEMENT

He that hath no rule over his own spirit is like a city that is broken down, and without walls (PROVERBS 25:28).

Every Christian man needs to learn to be a good manager of his own life. Managing oneself effectively eliminates one of the major causes of stress. Thank God we have within us by the Holy Spirit the ability to manage our lives successfully. That is, *if* we're managing what God has called us to and not *more* than God has called us to.

Take a brief inventory of your life. Is it manageable? Manageable without stress? If the answer is no, consider prayerfully where to cut loose time-robbing activities that are not as productive as others. If the answer is yes, consider how you may have time to help take on some responsibilities of others—including family members.

Manage well, live well, and finish well.

"We can easily manage if we will only take, each day, the burden appointed to it. But the load will be too heavy for us if we carry yesterday's burden over again today, and then add the burden of the morrow before we are required to bear it."
—JOHN NEWTON

NO CONDEMNATION!

There is therefore now no condemnation to them which are in Christ Jesus, who walk not after the flesh, but after the Spirit. For the law of the Spirit of life in Christ Jesus hath made me free from the law of sin and death (ROMANS 8:1-2).

Satan is a reality, and we must not be unaware of his devices and strategies for our fall. But to be honest, most men are more likely to fall into sin or even apathy from their own fleshly desires than from Satan's enticements. Christian men can and must become winners in the battle between their flesh and their desire to live holy and wholly. If the apostle Paul fought this battle (see Romans 7), we can be sure we will too. Temptation and sin are not unique to each of us. We are all prone to obey the flesh's siren call. But we must remember Paul won his battle, and so can we.

"What ground is left for accusation since sin's penalty has been fully paid? The blood of the Lord has atoned for all the sins of a believer; hence there is no more condemnation in the conscience." —WATCHMAN NEE

GOD'S UNSEEN HAND

That the trial of your faith, being much more precious than of gold that perisheth, though it be tried with fire, might be found unto praise and honor and glory at the appearing of Jesus Christ (1 PETER 1:7).

Happy is the man who perceives the unseen hand of God in every aspect of his life. Nothing can touch us that does not pass through the knowledge of God first. And when embraced by faith in God's goodness and His ability to work out His perfect plan for our lives, even trials turn to gold eventually. Trust in the unseen hand of God today. Just as He is always present, even when we don't perceive His presence, so too is He always at work even when we're unaware.

"When all nature is at rest, not a leaf moving, then at evening the dew comes down—no eye to see the pearly drops descending, no ear to hear them falling on the verdant grass—so does the Spirit come to you who believe. When the heart is at rest in Jesus—unseen, unheard by the world—the Spirit comes, and softly fills the believing soul, quickening all, renewing all within." —ROBERT MURRAY MCCHEYNE

Our Eternal Deposits

He that hath a bountiful eye shall be blessed; for he giveth of his bread to the poor (Proverbs 22:9).

What would it be like if every Christian would look upon money as something he gives more than something he earns or spends? Welfare as we know it might cease. Missionaries would have better tools to reach the lost. The homeless could find shelter. Happy is the man who isn't a slave to mammon but instead searches out new ways to give—often anonymously. If we would be good investors of our money, we would find there is no greater investment than the eternal deposits we make in our heavenly retirement account.

"Do not think me mad. It is not to make money that I believe a Christian should live. The noblest thing a man can do is just humbly to receive, and then go amongst others and give."
—David Livingstone

Our Ever-Present God

We love him, because he first loved us (1 John 4:19).

Though we may think we have searched for God and found Him in Christ, the truth is before we searched for Him, He searched for us and found us. He wanted us from day one in eternity past, and He wants us for every day in eternity future. We are His. He is ours. We are engraved on the palms of His hands. He is always with us and always *for* us.

"I am graven on the palms of His hands. I am never out of His mind. All my knowledge of Him depends on His sustained initiative in knowing me. I know Him, because He first knew me, and continues to know me. He knows me as a friend, One who loves me; and there is no moment when His eye is off me, or His attention distracted for me, and no moment, therefore, when His care falters." —J.I. Packer

PERSECUTION

Blessed are they which are persecuted for righteousness' sake: for theirs is the kingdom of heaven. Blessed are ye, when men shall revile you, and persecute you, and shall say all manner of evil against you falsely, for my sake. Rejoice, and be exceeding glad: for great is your reward in heaven: for so persecuted they the prophets which were before you (MATTHEW 5:10-12).

A Christian need not look for opposition—it will surely find him. It has always been so and will continue in the future, perhaps with an accelerated pace. The time to prepare for opposition isn't at the moment of confrontation but much earlier. In fact, *now* is always the best time to prepare for opposition.

There are two ways to prepare. One is to consider the opposition, scorn, and rejection the Lord Jesus went through for us. The second way is to focus on eternity, where all opposition will no longer exist. There is, then, an end to opposition, though there is not an end to our lives in Christ.

"If you are going to walk with Jesus Christ, you are going to be opposed. In our days, to be a true Christian is really to become a scandal."—GEORGE WHITEFIELD

THINK ON THESE THINGS

Finally, brethren, whatsoever things are true, whatsoever things are honest, whatsoever things are just, whatsoever things are pure, whatsoever things are lovely, whatsoever things are of good report; if there be any virtue, and if there be any praise, think on these things (PHILIPPIANS 4:8).

It is right to hate evil. But it's not right to focus so much on hating evil that we fail to love and approve that which is good. Some men are temperamentally predisposed to look for the half-empty glass, to expect the worst, to find fault. Sometimes our words of negativity are out of our mouths before we realize how unnecessary it was to offer our opinion. Speak that which is good. Think of the best things. See the glass not half empty nor half full but overflowing with the goodness of God. For each of us, our cup truly runs over.

"Our souls must not merely hate what is evil; we must love what is good." —THOMAS CHALMERS

OVERCOMING FAILURE

My flesh and my heart faileth: but God is the strength of my heart, and my portion for ever (PSALM 73:26).

If you've ever experienced colossal failure—and who hasn't—you know the aftermath is one of life's occasions when our flesh and our heart faileth. Our spirits couldn't be lower. We forget failure is the road to success.

For every man who reaches the pinnacle of success, there are others who, having failed, gave up their dreams. The difference between the two is that the former didn't fear failure; they knew that failure had its purpose in their quest, and they persisted despite failure after failure. Essentially, these men failed their way to success. The latter—those who have given up—couldn't see past their present or past failures to try again. Sometimes failure produces fear of future failure and stops the man in his tracks. Try. Fail. Try. Fail. Succeed. It's the way God brings us to maturity and allows us to see our dreams fulfilled.

"Trying, failing, and trying again is called learning."
—HENRY CLOUD

BE GLAD AND LAUGH!

Then was our mouth filled with laughter, and our tongue with singing: then said they among the heathen, The LORD hath done great things for them (PSALM 126:2).

Laughter is one of God's greatest gifts to man. A man who can find the humor in life—especially in life's darker moments—has God on his side. An easy laugh comes from a heart that is perpetually *glad*. If we are without gladness of heart, it can be cultivated. How? One place to start is ruminating on the goodness of God. Calling to mind the ways God has worked in our past to bring about a desired end. Another way to cultivate gladness of heart is to simply practice praising God no matter the circumstances. God is no less God during our rough patches than He is during our mountaintop experiences. Rejoice and be glad, Christian man! You are the possessor of all good things!

"Be glad and laugh from the low bottom of thine own heart."
—WILLIAM TYNDALE

Our One True Commitment

Seek ye first the kingdom of God, and his righteousness; and all these things shall be added unto you (Matthew 6:33).

We men are most likely to be successful at that to which we're totally committed. The problem is that many men try to be committed to too many things. We can only be totally committed to one thing to be effective. There are, of course, lesser commitments we make in life, but the one true commitment to which all other commitments must bow is our commitment to Christ. We must have a single eye for Him and His kingdom. When our curiosity suggests new commitments, we must make sure they won't supplant or diminish our one true commitment. We must weigh carefully new interruptions in our lives and consider whether they will hinder or help our one true commitment. All the important things in life will be added to us if we will seek first Christ and His kingdom.

"None do seek the Lord so earnestly, but they have need of stirring up to seek him more earnestly; neither have any attained to such a measure of communion with God, but they have need to seek for a further measure." —David Dickson

Nick Harrison is the author of several books, including these in the One-Minute Prayers® series from House Publishers:

One-Minute Prayers® for Husbands

The very best way you can take care of your wife is by praying for her and your marriage. Discover biblical encouragement in this collection of prayers and devotions written for busy husbands like you who need a minute of inspiration.

One-Minute Prayers® for Dads

Take a minute out of your day to thank God for your children, and let Him equip you for the challenges of fatherhood with these brief but powerful prayers that fit into your busy schedule.

One-Minute Prayers® for Those with Cancer

These writings will lead you from fear to faith in the face of illness. Each entry includes a reassuring encouragement as well as a suggested prayer to open your heart to nourishment and understanding.

One-Minute Prayers® When You Need a Miracle

When life looks bleak and you need God to show up in a big way, these prayers will connect your needs to God's promises, increase your faith, and enlarge your view of God.